Pathways
to
Responsibility

A Responsibility, Character Education, and
Violence Prevention Curriculum for Grade One

Donnita Weddle and Marian Adams

Learning Publications, Inc.
Holmes Beach, Florida

ISBN 1-55691-212-9

Learning Publications, Inc.
5351 Gulf Drive
P.O. Box 1338
Holmes Beach, FL 34218-1338

Printing: 5 4 3 2 1   Year: 05 04 03 02 01

Printed in the United States of America

Contents

Our Promise to You vi

Animal Characters Greet You vii

Learning Responsibility

Lesson 1 – Taking Responsibility 1

Lesson 2 – Responsibility 7

Being Special

Lesson 3 – I Am Special 10

Lesson 4 – Special Play 14

Kindness and Cooperation

Lesson 5 – Kindness 17

Lesson 6 – Cooperation..21

Lesson 7 – Obey Parents 25

Lesson 8 – Honesty 30

Self-Control

Lesson 9 – Self-Control 35

Lesson 10 – Anger Management 40

Listening

Lesson 11 – Listening 46

Lesson 12 – Listening Skit...49

Problem Solving

Lesson 13 – "I" Messages..52

Lesson 14 – Seeing Both Sides 55

Lesson 15 – Resolving Conflicts Peacefully...59

Empathy

Lesson 16 – Friendship 63

Lesson 17 – Playing Fair..66

Lesson 18 – Feeling Left Out...70

Coping

Lesson 19 – Refusal Skills 74

Lesson 20 – Handling Bullies 77

Lesson 21 – Having a Bad Day 81

Decision Making

Lesson 22 – Making Good Choices 85

Lesson 23 – We Can Learn From Our Mistakes 89

Goal Setting

Lesson 24 – Setting Goals 93

Appendices

Appendix A – How to Make Sock Puppets 96

Appendix B – Resource Sheets 98

Appendix C – Responsibility Contract 101

Acknowledgments

Thanks to Donnita's daughter, Kimberly Eileen Weddle, for giving encouragement to meet the challenge and accomplish the goal of writing this curriculum.

Thanks to Stan Davis, Sunnyside School District, Sunnyside, Wash., for his trust and belief that helped cultivate the education, experience, and confidence that made the creation of this curriculum possible.

Thanks also to the students of Lapwai Elementary, Lapwai, Ida.; Sunnyside School District, Sunnyside, Wash.; Culdesac School District, Culdesac, Ida.; Sacajawea Junior High and Lewiston High School, Lewiston, Ida. Through their participation they contributed to the creation of this curriculum.

A special thanks to friend and professional artist Bill Schreib who took our concepts of the Sunshine Elementary characters and made them real.

About the Authors

Donnita Weddle, M.S.ED/Counseling, B.S. Elementary ED, B.S. Criminal Corrections, A.A. in Behavioral Science, has been a teacher and counselor for many years, and also has researched a responsibility, character education, and violence-prevention curriculum for classroom guidance. She found she had to go to dozens of sources to put together a complete set of teaching materials, this brought about the awareness of the need for one resource that would cover all aspects of responsibility, character education, and violence prevention. In addition to counseling and teaching in these areas, Ms. Weddle has helped various schools set up playground conflict-management programs by training students and staff in the skills needed for peer mediation. Because of her expertise, she was invited to publish an article on the subject in the *Washington Learner* in 1994 entitled "Playground Conflict Peer Managers Prove Tremendous Benefit."

Marian Adams, A.A. and B.A. English/journalism with history, social studies, and reading additional certification, was Teacher of the Year in 1991, and the Lewiston City Commission member for Public Education Government Channel 13. She has been a journalism and English secondary teacher for 21 years and was aware of the need for students to learn responsibility and violence prevention at a young age so they may practice it in their teenage years. She has also traveled to England, China, and Germany observing education methods in those countries and lecturing on American journalism education.

Our Promise to You

We agree with parents, teachers, counselors, and administrators — children are special. Children need to be cherished and loved but they also need to learn to grow up to be responsible adults. We give you our promise that you can help children learn to cope with the feelings and problems all of us must face in this modern world while still nurturing their fragile psyches and creative spirits. If we, with your help, can get across to the child the 10 principles of being responsible adults, then we will have given our children a truly great gift. The children need to feel and act with the following principles as their guide to developing good character:

① I am special.

② Everyone is special and I give respect to everyone.

③ I am a good listener and have empathy.

④ I am honest.

⑤ I can make good decisions.

⑥ I can solve problems without violence.

⑦ I set goals.

⑧ Although it is not always easy, I can cope with whatever I need to cope with.

⑨ Although I make mistakes, I am willing to learn.

⑩ I am responsible for my own behavior.

The formative years are important. Preschool and primary school children need to get a good base in living, feeling, and believing all 10 of these principles. We, as teachers, must always remember in the teaching of these principles that in the creative child is often the dream and innovation for the future.

One of the best ways for young children to learn these principles is by seeing examples of them being used. Parents and teachers should provide the examples by their words and actions. This is not always possible. Therefore, the school must reinforce and teach these principles.

To help teachers teach these principles, this primary-grade curriculum on responsibility, character education, and violence prevention has been prepared. It contains stories and activities for children in first grade.

Animal Characters Greet You

Setting – Anytown, U.S.A.; Sunshine Elementary School

Characters:

- Lilly Lambkin – White, woolly lamb, a main character, twin sister to Lucky
- Lucky Lambkin – Black, woolly lamb, main character, twin brother to Lilly
- Ronnie Rabbit – Helpful floppy-eared rabbit
- Susie Squirrel – Curious brown, bushy-tailed squirrel (always grooming her tail)
- Doolee Dog – Full of mischief, somewhat of a bully
- Daisy Dog – Doolee's younger sister
- Cherry Chicken – Cheerleader type, happy and outgoing
- Ted Turkey – Fun-loving but likes to learn
- Minnie Moo – Shy and reserved
- Mabell Moo – Minnie's big sister who helps care for Minnie
- Corky Colt – High-spirited and full of fun
- Kathy Kat – Sympathetic, cares about others
- Billy Goat – A bit of a bully
- Tiny Tiger – Visitor from Africa to Sunshine Elementary

Adults:

- Teacher Mrs. Owl – Kind, considerate, knowledgeable, wise, first-grade teacher of Lilly's class
- Teacher Miss Lion – Enjoys children, kind, knowledgeable, Lucky's first-grade exchange teacher from Africa
- Various mothers as needed

Animal Characters Greet You at Sunshine Elementary 1st Grade

Lilly Lambkin

Lucky Lambkin

Ronnie Rabbit

Susie Squirrel

Doolee Dog

Daisy Dog

Cherry Chicken

Ted Turkey

Minnie Moo

Mabell Moo

Corky Colt

Kathy Kat

Billy Goat

Tiny Tiger

Mrs. Owl

Miss Lion

☑ Lesson 1: Taking Responsibility

> Taking Responsibility — Taking responsibility for your behavior means to accept the obligation of being accountable for how you act and what you do.

Being responsible is an obligation. When we are babies we don't have any obligations or any responsibility because our parents are responsible for us and see that we get fed and cared for. As we grow up, we begin to have responsibility for our clothes, our rooms, our pets, our school work, our feelings, our behavior, our choices in life. Even though sometimes we are busy playing, we still have to remember to be responsible for our chores. Being responsible for our behavior isn't always easy. Sometimes we have to work at it, but we also get the credit and praise when we do things that are good. Being responsible for our choices and behavior is very important because it helps us build good character as we grow.

Instructions (read to the students): We are going to begin a series of lessons that will teach us about being responsible in many areas of our lives. In these lessons we will meet many interesting characters who will be learning these lessons along with us as they attend the first grade at Sunshine Elementary School in Anytown, U.S.A. We will have many exciting adventures with these warm, lovable students who do many of the same things we do and face many of the same problems we have. Since they are not always perfect and neither are we, we will discover how they learn to solve problems, cope with life, and learn responsibility.

Characters: Introduce the characters to the students. Show pictures of the characters when describing them. Lilly Lambkin is a white, woolly girl lamb. Lucky Lambkin is a black, woolly boy lamb. Ronnie Rabbit is the Lambkins' friend and is a very helpful rabbit. Susie Squirrel is also a Lambkin friend and she is a very curious squirrel. (Refer to Animal Characters Greet You. If intending to make puppets, now would be the time to have a work session on the puppets — see instructions for Making Sock Puppets in Appendix A.)

Directions: After reading and discussing the introduction and the characters, briefly discuss some examples of responsible behavior. (Do chores at home, work at school, obey parents, be honest, help others, and admit if we break a rule, rather than blaming others.) If using puppets, select students to represent the characters in the story. After giving out the puppets, explain that when they hear their character (puppet) talk in the story, they are to raise the puppet so the other students can see which animal is talking. Tell students to listen to the story so they will be able to tell what Lucky Lambkin, Ronnie Rabbit, and Doolee Dog learned about taking responsibility for their behavior.

Taking Responsibility

One Saturday morning Lucky Lambkin, Ronnie Rabbit, and Doolee Dog were watching television in Doolee's living room. His mother, Mrs. Dog, had taken his sister, Daisy, to dance lessons and shopping and would be gone about two hours. Mrs. Dog instructed the youngsters to get Doolee's older brother, Duncan, if they needed anything. Duncan was upstairs in his room working on his computer. Then she set out some chocolate chip cookies for the boys and told Doolee there was a pitcher of strawberry punch in the refrigerator. Mrs. Dog cautioned Doolee that the boys must eat in the kitchen because she had recently had the living room carpet cleaned and didn't want them to drink the punch in there.

"I promise we will eat in the kitchen," Doolee had said. "You can trust me."

His mother had smiled and said, "Yes, Doolee, you are getting bigger and more responsible every day. That's why I let you have Lucky and Ronnie over to play." Then she left with Daisy.

The boys ate the cookies and had some punch in the kitchen before they went into the living room to watch television. They watched several programs, then their all-time favorite, the Ninja show, came on and they were absolutely glued to the television.

At the commercial, Ronnie said, "I'm thirsty. Let's have some more punch."

Doolee said, "Okay, but we have to go into the kitchen to drink it. I promised my mother we wouldn't bring it in here."

All the boys ran to the kitchen and Doolee passed around the punch. They were busy drinking it when they heard the Ninjas come back on and realized the commercial was over and their program had started again.

Doolee said, "Come on, let's go stand in the doorway and watch." They did. The program got really exciting and they all jumped up and down trying to imitate the Ninjas. They began crashing into each other.

"Watch out," said Ronnie, "we better stop." So Ronnie and Lucky took their drinks back to the kitchen while Doolee took his punch into the living room.

Doolee was being silly and kept jumping and kicking like a Ninja. Just as he decided he better get back to the kitchen with his punch, it finally swirled around in the glass and sloshed over the edge. "Zowwee!" Doolee yelled as punch went all over him and the carpet.

Doolee just stood there, looking sick."

The boys all grabbed dishtowels and started mopping up the mess. There were several big red spots on the light blue carpet.

"It's not coming out," wailed Doolee. "Mom'll be really mad."

"Come on, keep working," said Lucky. "Let's wet the towels and see if we can rub the stains out."

The more they rubbed the carpet with the wet towels the bigger the spots got. Finally, Ronnie sat back on his heels and said, "It's never going to come out. Your mom won't ever let us come over again."

"What will I do?" asked Doolee, ready to cry.

"I know," said Lucky. "Let's move that table over it."

"Don't be silly," said Doolee. "That has a light on it."

"Move the light, too," Ronnie said.

So that's what the boys did. The table with the light on it looked a bit funny since it was sticking out into the living room doorway.

The boys didn't really enjoy watching the rest of their program.

When the program was over, they decided to go outside and play in the backyard for a while but they weren't having fun because they were still worried.

"You can go home if you want," Doolee told Ronnie and Lucky.

The two boys said they would stay and help him tell his mother about the accident.

Just then, Mrs. Dog drove up and she and Daisy got out of the car. The three boys went quickly to the car and offered to help carry the groceries. Mrs. Dog thanked them and thought how nice and considerate the boys were.

As they all walked in, Daisy ran into the living room and almost tripped over the light and table.

"Why is that table there?" asked Mrs. Dog.

"I don't know," said Doolee.

Mrs. Dog, being like most mothers, was pretty smart so she went over and moved the table and saw the spots. They had faded quite a bit but they were still noticeable. "What happened here?" She asked.

"I don't know," said Doolee. He wanted to tell her but just couldn't because he knew she would never trust him again.

"I think you do know. Boys, what happened?" asked Mrs. Dog.

All three boys hung their heads looking very guilty.

Lucky said, "Mom's expecting me. I have to go home."

"Me, too," said Ronnie and both boys practically ran out the door.

"Well, that was a fast retreat," said Mrs. Dog. "I guess it's up to you to explain, Doolee."

Doolee hung his head and considered blaming it all on his friends since they were gone but he looked at his mother and thought, I have to take responsibility for this or mom won't ever trust me again. So he said, "We got excited over the Ninja program and were making the Ninja moves when the punch spilled."

"Doolee," Mrs. Dog asked, "What were the three of you doing in the living room?"

"Well, we weren't all in the living room, Mom . . . just me," Doolee admitted.

For a minute Mrs. Dog just looked at him. Then she said, "You know it was your responsibility to make sure the punch stayed in the kitchen. I should be very angry but I am proud of you for taking responsibility for your behavior."

"I am so sorry," Doolee said. "We tried to clean it up and it just got bigger. I don't know what to do about it."

"I have some rug cleaner that you can use to scrub the spots," said Mrs. Dog and she went to the closet and got it out. "You will have to dip this rag in the cleaner and rub it until the spots disappear."

Doolee worked hard and finally got the spots out. After his mother inspected the carpet, she said, "Doolee, sometimes accidents happen and we are tempted to try to cover them up or lie about them. What is important is that you were honest and accepted the responsibility for your behavior. Now, let's go out to the kitchen and you can help me make lunch."

⚠️? Discussion Questions

1. What does it mean "to take responsibility for your behavior"? (To be held accountable for your behavior.)

2. What happened in the story? (Doolee accidentally spilled punch on the carpet.)

3. Why was the spilled punch a problem? (It got spots on the carpet and the boys couldn't get them out.)

4. Did Lucky and Ronnie take any responsibility? (Yes, they tried to help Doolee clean the carpet.)

5. Whose responsibility was it to stay out of the living room? (Doolee had told his mother he would keep the boys out of the living room.)

6. What was Doolee thinking about telling his mother? (Doolee was thinking about telling his mom that his friends had spilled the punch.)

7. What could Doolee have done to prevent the accident? (He could have drank his punch in the kitchen.)

8. How did Doolee finally take responsibility? (He told his mother that he caused the accident.)

🎭 Activities

1. Have students tell about a time when they were tempted to avoid taking responsibility for their behavior.

2. Draw and color a picture of a time when students took responsibility for their behavior and share the picture with the class.

🙇 Role Play

How would you practice taking responsibility for your behavior if . . .

1. You accidentally broke a lamp in your house when you and your friends were playing. Mom wants to know what happened.

2. You forgot to feed the fish in the aquarium and they died. Your sister wants to know what happened to the fish.

3. You let the dog out of the yard as you went to a friend's house and it got lost. Dad wants to know how the dog got out.

4. You forgot the time and stayed too long playing at a friend's house. You have to explain to your mom.

5. You found a coat laying in the school play yard and you were cold so you wore it home. Dad wants to know where you got the coat.

6. You and your friend found a dollar in the street in front of your house. What will you do with the dollar?

7. The salesclerk only charged you $1.50 for something you bought that cost $2.50.

8. Your friend took a candy bar at the store and didn't pay for it when the two of you left the store.

9. Your brother and you found some candy just laying on your sister's books in the hallway.

10. You ate some of the cake your mother made to take to the bake sale. She wants to know what happened to it.

11. You forgot to remind your mother to make cupcakes for your class for the party the next day.

☑ Lesson 2: Responsibility

> Responsibility — Responsibility is when we accept the obligation of being dependable and trustworthy and are accountable for our behavior.

To take responsibility is to show that we are someone who can be trusted and can be counted on to take care of our obligations and duties. If we are put in charge of chores around the house or the care of a brother, sister, or a pet, we are expected to be responsible for these jobs. Sometimes we have duties outside the house, like at school when we are expected to complete assignments on time and follow school rules. This is our job. It is important to show that we are a dependable person and that we can be trusted by our parents and teachers to take responsibility for our behavior. Sometimes we make mistakes and here, too, we must take responsibility and help correct the mistake, not blame others for it. Doing this helps us build good character.

Directions: Read and discuss the introduction above and review what students have already learned about responsibility. Have students name examples of responsible behavior. (Do chores at home, work at school, obey parents, be honest, help others, and admit if we break a rule, rather that blaming others.) If using puppets, select students to represent the characters in the story. After giving out the puppets, explain that when they hear their character (puppet) talk in the story, they are to raise the puppet so the other students can see which animal is talking. Tell students to listen to the story so they will be able to tell what the animal friends learn about responsibility.

Who Is Responsible?

One Monday morning after Mrs. Owl's first-grade class finished the pledge of allegiance to the flag she told the children that she had a poem to read to them about Little Boy Blue. Please listen to the poem then we will discuss if Little Boy Blue took care of his responsibilities.

Now listen carefully:

> Little Boy Blue, come blow your horn.
> The sheep's in the meadow,
> The cow's in the corn.
> Where's the little boy who looks after the sheep?
> He's under the haystack, fast asleep.

The children all laughed but Kathy Kat didn't.

"Why aren't you laughing, Kathy?" asked Mrs. Owl.

"Because the poor sheep could get lost and the cow could eat all the corn and get sick," said Kathy.

"That's right," said Mrs. Owl. "Who was responsible for taking care of the sheep and cow?"

Lilly Lambkin looked at Kathy and held up her hand.

(The teacher stops reading and asks the following questions.)

1. Who is Lilly going to say is responsible for taking care of the animals? (Little Boy Blue)

2. Are the sheep responsible for staying in the meadow? Would they get lost? (The sheep only care about eating grass so may wander out of the meadow and may get lost. Sheep do not have a sense of responsibility. Most animals don't have a sense of responsibility but are like babies in that someone must care for them.)

3. What may happen if the cow stays in the corn field? (The cow might eat too much corn and get sick and the people who own the corn field may not have enough corn to eat or sell.)

4. Why is Little Boy Blue supposed to take care of the animals? (Because it's his job.)

(The teacher goes back to the story.)

After Mrs. Owl called on her, Lilly said, "Little Boy Blue was responsible. He should have stayed awake and watched the sheep and cow."

"Good answer." "That's correct," said Mrs. Owl.

The children discussed responsibility a bit more then Mrs. Owl said, "How do you think Little Boy Blue will feel? Let's find out. I will read you the poem again, this time adding the last three lines." So she did.

Little Boy Blue, come blow your horn.
The sheep's in the meadow,
The cow's in the corn.
Where is the boy who looks after the sheep?
He's under the haystack, fast asleep.
Will you wake him?
No, not I.
For if I do, he's sure to cry.

After Mrs. Owl read the poem, the students discussed the last three lines and so will the students in our classroom.

⚠ Discussion Questions

1. Why won't they wake up Little Boy Blue? (They think he will cry.)

2. Why do they think he will cry? (He is not doing his job.)

3. How do you think Little Boy Blue will feel? Why? (Lead students into a discussion about feeling upset because he was not responsible and may feel that people won't trust him any more.)

4. What should Little Boy Blue do after he wakes up? (He should blow his horn, get the cow out of the corn, and check that all the sheep are there.)

5. Should Little Boy Blue admit his mistake? Why? (Yes, lead students into discussion about taking responsibility for mistakes and trying to make up for them.)

6. Tell of a time you made a mistake and didn't do a chore or task that you were supposed to do and what happened.

🏃 Role Play

What would you do in the following situations . . .

1. It is your job to clean your room and a friend calls you to go to a movie.

2. You are in charge of watching your little brother and a neighbor wants you to come outside and play ball.

3. You have to deliver the evening newspapers and a friend invites you over to eat pizza.

4. Your dog is whining for her food and water and your favorite television show is starting.

5. You have a science project due tomorrow and your friend wants you to spend the night.

6. You are responsible for cleaning the white board at recess, but all the guys are going straight out to play the soccer championship game.

7. You took out the class basketball at recess, but as the bell rang to go in you saw a girl from another class taking it inside.

8. You and a friend were playing ball in the house and you knocked your mom's favorite picture off the wall and broke the glass.

9. You and your sister were drinking milk in the living room and you knocked your glass off the coffee table and it spilled all over the carpet.

10. You were in the middle of playing a fun game at a friend's house when it was time to go home.

✓ Lesson 3: I Am Special

Special — Everyone is valuable and unique (special).
Being special is knowing that no one else looks like you,
no one else talks like you, no one else thinks like you.
You are one of a kind.

You know you are special because no one else has the same nose, fingernails, or fingerprints. No one else has the exact same color of hair. No one else has the same shape or color of eyes. No one else has the same shape or size of hands, feet, or toes. No one else has the same place in your family. No one else has the same talents and abilities you have. We are all special and valuable and we are each in charge of our own feelings. It is our responsibility to help mend our hurt feelings by telling ourselves that we are special and telling one thing we are good at doing.

Directions: Read and discuss the introduction and have students name some examples of responsible behavior. (Do chores at home, work at school, obey parents, be honest, help others, and admit if we break a rule rather than blaming others.) Ask what responsibility has to do with being special. (Be sure to emphasize that it is our responsibility to take care of ourselves and our feelings by telling ourselves that we are special and telling one thing we are good at doing.) For the lesson, if using puppets, select four students to represent the characters in the story. After giving out the puppets, explain that when they hear their character (puppet) talk in the story, they are to raise the puppet so the other students can see which animal is talking. Explain the characters to the students (if not previously introduced): Lilly Lambkin is a white, woolly girl lamb. Lucky Lambkin is a black, woolly boy lamb. Ronnie Rabbit is the Lambkins' friend and is a very helpful rabbit. Susie Squirrel is also a Lambkin friend and she is a very curious squirrel. (The teacher may want to teach "I Am Special" song now which is sung to "Brother John" tune, see Appendix B, Resource Sheet 1.) Tell the students to listen to the story so they will be able to tell what Lucky Lambkin learned about being special. Read the story.

I Am Special

Lilly Lambkin came rushing into the house with her twin brother, Lucky, lagging behind. School was out and it was Friday but Lilly could see that Lucky had an unhappy look on his face.

"What's wrong with you?" Lilly asked.

"Nothin'," said Lucky as he hung his woolly head and pushed out his lower lip.

"Come on, tell me what's wrong," said his twin sister. "Did you get into trouble at school?"

"Why do you always think I get into trouble? Miss Lion likes me and says I am good at helping others." But Lucky's lower lip was still hanging down.

"Let's have the milk and cookies that mom left out," Lilly said thinking maybe she could distract her brother.

Just as the two little lambs finished their milk and cookies, they heard a thumping at the door.

"Oh, look, it's Ronnie Rabbit," Lilly yelled as she opened the door for their friend.

"Hi," said Ronnie as he hopped into the kitchen. He looked at Lucky and immediately figured out something was wrong and said to Lucky, "What's your trouble?"

"Nothin'," answered Lucky again.

Just then they heard a scratching at the window. It was their friend, Susie Squirrel. Lilly ran to the window and opened it, giggling as she tickled Susie between her ears.

Susie laughed, wiggling her head, "Hi, Lambkins, what did you do in school today?"

"I had a great day," said Lilly. Then she looked at her brother because his head was hanging again and his lower lip stuck out, "but Lucky looks sad and won't tell me why. Something must have happened to him at school because he was happy this morning."

"Oh, Lucky, what's wrong?" asked Susie, who was very curious.

"Yes, tell us. We are your friends and we want to help you," said Ronnie as he put his hand on Lucky's arm to comfort him.

"Aw, I don't want to tell you," Lucky said shyly.

"We love you and think you are great," Lilly said in an effort to get her brother to tell them the problem.

"Yeah," Susie squeaked, jumping up and down. "We want to help."

"Well, today at recess Doolee Dog and Corky Colt never asked me play ball with them. They never even looked at me and I really wanted to play ball," said Lucky sadly. "Probably nobody wants to play with me any more."

"Don't be silly," said Susie. "You are a great person and you are special. You know sometimes kids are busy playing and don't even see their other friends but that doesn't mean they don't like them any more. That just means they are paying attention to their game."

"Really?" asked Lucky. "I guess I did get out to recess a little late because I stopped to help Cherry Chicken with spelling and by the time I got to the playground, Doolee and Corky were already in the middle of a game of catch."

"See," shouted Ronnie. "You're great to help Cherry with her spelling. Besides Mrs. Owl has been teaching us that we are all special so I know you're special, Lucky!"

"Yeah," said Lilly. "Our teacher taught us that we're each one of a kind. She said that when we get our feelings hurt, we can say something we're good at and remind ourselves how special we are. Mrs. Owl even taught us a song about being special. Here, I'll teach it to your guys. Come on, help me, Ronnie." (Special song is sung to "Brother John" tune — can be sung as round.)

> I am special.
> I am special.
>
> So are you.
> So are you.
>
> Always remember.
> Always remember.
>
> This is true.
> This is true.

After Lilly and Ronnie sang it once, Lilly asked the others to sing it too. Then all four friends started singing the song.

*(Stop here and have the students sing the "I Am Special" song,
see Appendix B, then continue reading.)*

By the time they were done singing, the friends were all giggling.

Lucky said, "I like that little song and you know I feel lots better now. I guess you're right. I am special and probably Doolee and Corky were just too busy to notice me. But even if they weren't, it's all right because I know I'm special and I am also a super, terrific, helpful friend."

"Good for you!" said Ronnie.

"Enough of this stuff," Susie said. "Why don't you all come out and play with me. We can all play catch until it's time for dinner."

"Yeah, let's go!" Lucky yelled as they all raced out to play.

⚠ Discussion Questions

1. Why was Lucky unhappy? (His friends didn't invite him to play.)
2. What happened to make Lucky feel better? (He talked to his friends.)

3. What did Lucky say to himself at the end? (I'm special and I'm good at helping others.)

4. Tell about a time when you felt you were not special. What did you do to make yourself feel better?

5. Next time, what could you do to make yourself feel special again? (Talk to someone about it, tell yourself you are special, tell yourself what you are good at doing, work on a hobby and/or go play.)

Activities

1. Have students draw a picture of a time when they felt they were special.

2. Have the students brainstorm specific things they are good at doing. (List them on the board.) Have each student name something they can tell themselves when they need to feel good (e.g., I am good at math, reading, spelling, hitting a ball, catching a ball, cooking, sewing, swimming, etc.).

Role Play

Have students role play some of the following situations. (Direct the role plays so that students tell themselves something they are good at doing and they are special.)

1. Susie forgot to invite you to her birthday party.

2. Bill and Tom didn't invite you to play at recess.

3. Angie and Sara were telling secrets and not including you.

4. Todd shared his candy with Larry and left you out.

5. You asked Linda for a turn on the swing and she gave it to Jill.

6. Rob wouldn't let you sit by him at lunch.

7. Sally wouldn't sit with you on the bus.

8. Bobby took the basketball out at recess and wouldn't let you play.

9. Judy and Lynn wouldn't let you play jump rope.

10. The class was having free time and Mike wouldn't let you color with him.

☑ **Lesson 4: Special Play**

> Special — Everyone is valuable and unique.
> Each of us is different from all others.

Being special is knowing that no one else looks like you, no one else talks like you, no one else thinks like you. You are one of a kind. Each of us is special and valuable. You know you are special because no one else has the same nose that you do. No one else has the exact same color of hair. No one else has the fingernails and fingerprints. No one else has the same shape or color of eyes. No one else has the same shape of feet or toes. No one else has the same size hands. No one else has the same talents. Because each of us is special and valuable, each of us has the right to tell others to stop hurting us.

Directions: Review what it means to practice responsible behavior and have students give examples. (Do chores, do school work, help others, be honest, obey parents, admit when we break a rule rather than blaming others.) Ask students to discuss how responsibility relates to being special (because each of us is special we have the responsibility to stand up for ourselves and take care of ourselves and our feelings). Discuss with the students three things that are important to do to handle situations to keep feeling special even when being hurt:

1. Say "Stop it. I don't like it. It hurts me (or my feelings)."
2. Say "I am special."
3. If necessary, get help from someone you trust. The teacher may want to make some preparation for the following play by arranging to have adults or older students read the parts of each character. (A copy of the play should be made for the two characters.) Tell the students to listen to the play so they can tell if Lilly is able to handle the responsibility of taking care of herself and her feelings.

"Special" Play

Teacher reads the class the setting: All the children were walking out to the playground at Sunshine Elementary when Doolee ran past Lilly and slugged her on the arm.

Lilly:	Ouch! That hurt!
Doolee: (slugs her again)	Tough!
Lilly:	Why are you hitting me? Stop it. I don't like it when you hurt me.
Doolee:	You sissy.

Lilly:	I'm special. I shouldn't be hurt by anybody.
Doolee:	Yeah, yeah, yeah. Who says?
Lilly:	Mrs. Owl says everyone is special and doesn't have to put up with any kind of unwanted touching.
Doolee:	What does that have to do with me hitting you?
Lilly:	Well, I am special and hitting is an unwanted touch. I have the right to be here without having to worry about when you are going to come up and slug me.
Doolee:	Nan na nan na nan na! What are you going to do about it?
Lilly:	I remember what Mrs. Owl told us to do if someone is hurting us or trying to hurt us. She said we could run away or we could go tell an adult and get help.
Doolee:	What are you going to do?
Lilly:	I have some ideas of my own, too. I could also hit you back or get one of my friends to hit you. But, I think those are dumb ideas and would just get me into trouble.
Doolee:	Gee, I guess you do have some choices. I agree hitting me would just get us both into trouble and I sure don't want to get hit by anybody else.
Lilly:	That's right. I see that sometimes you hit people just for the fun of it. Don't you realize it hurts and keeps them from feeling special?
Doolee:	I guess I don't think about that.
Lilly:	Well, I'm special and I don't deserve to get hit. So, Doolee, what are we going to do about this?"
Doolee:	I don't know but I'm getting tired of talking about it. Would it help if I apologized and promise never to hit you again?
Lilly:	Sure, I accept your apology. I trust your promise because you are special, too.

⚠ Discussion Questions

1. What was happening to make Lilly lose her feelings of being special? (Doolee hit her.)

2. What did Lilly do when Doolee hit her? (She told Doolee to stop it and that she was too special to be hit.)

15

3. What did Lilly and Doolee decide to do? (They discussed what to do and Doolee apologized and promised not to hit her again.)

4. Was Lilly able to take responsibility for taking care of herself and her feelings? (Yes) How? (She said she was too special to be hit.)

5. Have you ever had a problem like Lilly's? What did you do? Did it work? Why or why not?

6. What can you do next time someone hits or hurts you? (Say "Stop it, I am special." And/or run away and get help.)

✗ Activity

Draw a picture of someone you would feel safe to tell if someone was hurting you, then color it.

✗ Role Play

Direct students to use the following in the role plays to help take care of their feelings and keep feeling special:

1. Say "Stop it. I don't like it. It hurts me (or my feelings)."
2. Say "I am special."
3. If necessary, get help from someone you trust.

How would the students take care of themselves and their feelings in the following situations . . .

1. Fred pulled Mary's hair when the teacher wasn't looking.
2. Lucy and Joan kept grabbing Tom at recess and kissing him.
3. John grabbed Susie in the hallway and hugged her.
4. Lou poked Milton with her pencil.
5. Rich and his friends laughed at Brenda and said they could see her underwear.
6. Pam kept telling Tom that he was her boyfriend and he didn't like it.
7. Henry grabbed Lori's clothes when she walked by his desk.
8. Ashley and Sara squirted water from the drinking fountain on Dawn.
9. Bill walked by and slugged Sue in the arm.
10. Breena twisted Shayla's finger.

☑ Lesson 5: Kindness

> **Kindness** — Kindness is the ability to do good, be gentle, tenderhearted and forgiving, and to help each other.

Being kind is thinking and considering the feelings of others. Sometimes it helps to think how you would feel if someone were unkind to you and did some things that hurt your feelings. Kindness has a lot to do with caring and showing it. Some of the people we care about and we can show kindness to are our family, friends, and neighbors. Kindness is treating other people like we want to be treated. It is everyone's responsibility to behave in a kind manner to all others and to take responsibility for our behavior when we don't. This helps us build character.

Directions: Read and discuss the introduction. Review the meaning of responsibility (being accountable for our behavior). Ask students to give some examples of responsible behavior. (Do chores, work at school, obey parents, be honest, help others, and admit if we break a rule, rather than blaming others.) Ask students how they think responsibility relates to kindness. (It is our responsibility to treat others with kindness and respect.) If using puppets, have students raise the puppets when they hear their character's name in the following story. Tell students to listen to the story so they can tell if Lilly, Cherry, and the others treat Minnie with kindness.

Lunch Time

All the students in Miss Lion's and Mrs. Owl's classes always enjoyed lunch time because it meant talking to their friends and having neat treats that their mothers packed in their lunches. Lilly Lambkin's friends always sat together.

"I have the best lunch today," said Cherry Chicken as she brought out her most favorite sandwich, a peanut butter and jam one.

"Hey, I've got one, too," said Lilly and both she and Cherry giggled.

"I've got chicken noodle soup in my thermos," said Susie Squirrel, "and it is really good."

"Look at my chocolate chip cookie," Kathy Kat said. "What have you got that's good in your lunch, Minnie?" Kathy asked.

"I've got to go back to the room, I forgot my lunch," said Minnie Moo as she headed to the lunch-room door. At the door, she told the teacher that she forgot her lunch and would be right back. But Minnie didn't come back to the lunch room. She met the others outside after lunch time and they all played together.

As the girls were walking back to the room after lunch hour, Lilly commented,"Did you notice that Minnie acts kind of sad?"

"Don't be silly," said Cherry. "Hurry, or we'll miss our place in line."

The next day, Minnie wasn't at school and her friends wondered where she was.

Friday, Minnie was back in school and told her friends that she had been sick. That day, too, Minnie forgot her lunch in the classroom and had to meet her friends later on the playground.

Then the next Monday, Minnie said she forgot her lunch again in the classroom and the same thing happened, but her friends talked about it and they decided that something was wrong.

"I don't think Minnie is happy," Lilly said. "I saw her crying after school the other day but when I came up to her and asked her, she said she had something in her eye."

"I don't think she really brings a lunch," said Susie. "Something must be going on."

"I have an idea," said Cherry. "Let's all bring something extra each day and see that she gets it to eat because I think she isn't eating."

"That's a good idea," the girls agreed.

Tuesday when Minnie said she forgot her lunch in the classroom, Lilly said, "Oh, just leave it. I have an extra sandwich and you can eat it and get your lunch later."

"I have an extra cookie," said Cherry.

"I have an extra apple my mother made me bring," said Susie.

"See, you can eat here then we can all go play sooner," said Lilly.

"Gee, thanks," said Minnie and it looked like she got something in her eye again.

After they all finished lunch, Minnie asked them if they wanted to go out on the playground and sit under the tree. "You are all so kind to me that I have something I want to share with you," she said.

When the girls were all settled, Lilly said, "We love you, Minnie. We know something is wrong. What can we do to help?"

Minnie started crying, "My parents are getting a divorce and dad has moved out and I'm so sad. We don't have any money for my lunch and I've been so hungry until today when you guys were so kind and gave me part of yours. You are so great. You are my best friends."

All the girls hugged Minnie and Cherry said, "We love you. You are our best friend and what happens to one of us happens to all of us. We have plenty of food and we want to share it with you just like we know you would do for us. You are special to us."

"You must believe that everything will work out," said Susie who always looks on the best side of things. "We will always be here for you until your mom gets a job or something good happens."

"Let's go jump rope," said Cherry and she grabbed hold of Minnie and the girls all went running to the jump-rope area.

⚠ Discussion Questions

1. What was Minnie doing at lunch time? (Saying she left her lunch in the room.)
2. Did the friends believe that Minnie had left her lunch in the classroom? (No)
3. What caused Lilly to suspect that Minnie was having problems? (She saw her crying.)
4. How were the friends kind to Minnie? (They decided to bring extra items in their lunch, they told her she was important and special to them.)
5. Tell about a time when you were kind to someone.
6. Tell about a time when someone was kind to you.

🏃 Activities

1. Have the students give examples of acts of kindness. (Helping mom or dad with chores, helping a friend learn a new game, share a toy, share food, lend a sweater, lend school supplies, etc.)
2. Draw a picture of yourself showing kindness to another person.
3. During the next room party, have students pick a favorite cookie and share it with someone.
4. Have students agree on a kindness project such as helping a family in the community or sending money to people in need.

⚹ Role Play

How would you show kindness in each of these situations . . .

1. Lynn is walking in front of you and accidentally drops her books.
2. Two of your friends were picking on a new kid in class.
3. At lunch time, Jimmy discovers he forgot his lunch.
4. A new student in your class was standing all by himself at recess.
5. Jane fell down and hurt her knee.
6. Susie and Jane were turning the jump rope too fast for Toni, the littlest in class, to jump and she kept falling down but kept trying.
7. Marie got her feelings hurt and she was crying.
8. Dawn is having trouble with math.
9. Joe and Frank were laughing at the new boy every time he said anything because he was from another area and talked differently.
10. Mom came home from work very tired.

☑ Lesson 6: Cooperation

Cooperation — Cooperation is the act
of working together; united effort.

Some things are too hard to do alone so sometimes we all have to work together to get the task done. This is called cooperation. Sometimes teachers want us to cooperate on projects because they think we need to practice our responsibility as a part of a team and work together with others. Cooperation isn't always easy because sometimes we think we know the answer and we want to be the one to get the credit. Sometimes we have to remember that everybody on the team or in the group has a right to express their opinion and help with the project or play in the game. When we take the responsibility to cooperate with others, we often find out that others have different ideas and sometimes they are very good ideas. We would never know this if we didn't cooperate, listen, and learn.

Directions: After reading and discussing the introduction, briefly discuss some examples of responsible behavior. (Do chores at home, work at school, obey parents, be honest, help others, and admit if we break a rule, rather than blaming others.) Ask students what practicing responsibility has to do with cooperation and working in a group or on a team. (It is our responsibility to cooperate and help our group or team.) If using puppets, select students to hold up the puppet when they hear their character's name mentioned in the story. Tell students you are going to read a story about first graders who will be working on a science project. They must listen carefully so they are able to discuss what happened when some group members did not cooperate.

Cooperation and a Science Project

Miss Lion's and Mrs. Owl's classes are going to get together and work on their science projects. The students in both classes are excited about the plans which included the students picking their own project groups.

Before the two classes got together, the teachers had asked the students to write down the names of three other students they would like to have in their groups. Then the exciting day came. The two classes got together and, surprise Lilly Lambkin was so happy because Susie Squirrel and Doolee Dog were in her group. So was Ted Turkey. Lucky Lambkin and Ronnie Rabbit were matched with Cherry Chicken and a new student in school, Minnie Moo. All the students were to do the same experiment and each group was to report the results to the class.

The experiment is so exciting, Lilly thought to herself as Miss Lion described what the students were to do. The students were to "discover" which of the objects each group was given would float in water.

Miss Lion told the students to first write down which objects they think will float and then do the experiment to see if they are right.

The teachers put the pan of water on the groups' desks and gave them the objects. Lilly's group got a cork, a pencil, a little piece of paper, an eraser, a small plastic ruler, a little bar magnet, a marble, a rubber ball, a paper clip, and a small plastic cup.

As soon as they sat down at the table, Doolee grabbed the ball and was tossing it up and down.

"Doolee, pay attention. We have to write down which things we think will float," Susie said as she took the pencil and started writing on the paper.

"Susie, we have to use that pencil and paper in the experiment," said Lilly. "Here, use mine."

Ted and Doolee were playing catch when the teacher looked over to their group and said, "Group No. 4, you need to concentrate and work together or you won't get your lesson done."

"See, you guys, you have already gotten us into trouble. Let's get busy. Which ones do you think will float?" asked Lilly.

The four, after discussing which one would float, finally agreed on all but the little plastic cup. The boys said it wouldn't float because it would fill up with water and sink and the girls said it would float if it was put in upside-down. They finally decided to write down that half of their group thought it would float.

Then came the big moment! They were ready to do the actual experiment where they would put the objects into the pan of water. In went the cork and it floated as they had guessed. Doolee picked up the eraser and threw it into the water, splashing Susie right in the face.

"Oh!" she exclaimed. "I am all wet! Quit goofing off, Doolee."

"You look funny all wet," Doolee said as he tossed in the ball for another big splash. "I'm just doing the experiment." With that he grabbed the marble and tossed it at the pan but he missed and it went rolling across the floor and he went scrambling after it.

Ted leaped up and ran after Doolee and the marble, too. The two boys bumped heads and Doolee said, "Watch out! Miss Lion will see us."

"Oh, she sees us and is coming over. We're in trouble," Ted said.

"Doolee! Ted! Why are you on the floor? Go over to the wall chairs and sit down until I can come talk to you," said Miss Lion as she worked with another group.

"Geez, we blew it, Doolee," said Ted.

"Yeah, we sure did," agreed Doolee. "Now we can't work with our group and they won't get done."

"Boy, I'll pay attention and work . . . if we can have another chance," said Ted.

Then Miss Lion came over. "What were you doing on the floor and why weren't you working with your group?" she asked.

"We dropped the marble and were chasing it and we got carried away," said Doolee.

"We're sorry. We won't do it again," said Ted.

"Well, boys, I hope you learned your lesson, but I'm not sure. What should you have been doing?"

"We should have been working with our group and helping each other rather than playing around," both boys agreed.

"Since you seem to have learned something, I will let you go back to your group," Miss Lion said.

"Wow, we were lucky," said Doolee ducking his head as Lilly glared at him.

"We're sorry; we got our group into trouble," said Ted.

"Yeah," agreed Doolee. "I think we need to cool it and get busy. It looks like some of the other groups are almost done and we want to do as good as they do."

"You're right," said Lilly and the boys started putting the objects into the water and reporting the results out loud. Then they switched and the girls put the objects in and reported. They all worked together rapidly to make up for the time they had not cooperated.

"Wow," said Lilly. "We're done just when everyone else is done. I'm glad we learned to work together."

"It's been fun," said Doolee. "I'm sorry I didn't know how important it is for a group to work a project together and cooperate. In fact, I didn't even know what cooperation meant and now I do."

After the teachers led a discussion about the results of the experiment and they all cleaned up, it was time for recess.

On the way out the door, Ted yelled, "Hey, guys, let's all go out and see if we can cooperate and play together in a game of kick ball."

"Yeah," they shouted as they headed for the play field.

⚠ Discussion Questions

1. What does cooperation mean? (Work together)
2. What activity were the classes doing that required the students to work together? (Science experiment)

3. Who was not cooperating? (Doolee and Ted)

4. What were they doing? (Goofing off)

5. What made them decide to start working as a group? (The teacher caught them and they learned it was important to help the group.)

6. Tell about a time you were working or playing in a group and one person would not cooperate? (Have some students respond to this question.) Have you ever been the uncooperative person in the group?

7. How did you feel when this happened? (frustrated, angry, upset, sad)

8. What did you do when they wouldn't cooperate?

9. Tell how Doolee and Ted learned their lesson?

🏃 Activities

1. Have students do the same experiment as the animal characters did and report the results.

2. Then have students tell whether or not their groups cooperated.

🧎 Role Play

How would you show cooperation if . . .

1. You and your sister were asked to clean the table and do the dishes.

2. Tony and you are asked to clean the white board.

3. You and your friends decide to play ball.

4. It is your classroom's turn to go outside to pick up playground litter and you have to walk beside Toby who always grabs things off the ground, even if they are in front of you.

5. You and your older sister have to babysit your little sister. Your older sister is busy and wants you to change the baby but you want to watch your favorite television show.

6. Your mother asks you and your brother to clean up the living room.

7. There is only one can of soda in the refrigerator and both you and your brother want it.

8. Your brother and you want to watch different programs on television.

9. Your sister and you have to sweep off the front sidewalk and there is only one broom.

10. You and a classmate have been asked to put away the classroom's crayons and clean the coloring table.

✓ Lesson 7: Obey Parents

Obey – Obey means to do what you are told. Parents are your guardians and they care about you and want to keep you safe. To obey your parents means to do what they ask you to do.

Most adults care about children, but your parents care most of all. Your responsibility is to obey your parents about safety rules, do your homework, come home on time, do your chores, and be considerate of others. That's a lot for first graders to remember, but it's important, so even though we sometimes make mistakes or forget about the time or don't get our homework done, we know our parents love us and will be upset that we did not obey them. It is our responsibility to try to remember to always follow our parents' rules.

Directions: Read and discuss the introduction. Review some examples of responsible behavior and ask what responsibility has to do with obeying your parents. (It is our responsibility to obey our parents.) If using puppets, chose students to represent the characters in the story and have them stand where they can be seen by the other students. After giving out the puppets, explain that when they hear their character (puppet) talk in the story, they are to raise the puppet so the other students can see which character is talking. Tell the students to listen carefully to the story so they can tell what some of the students at Sunshine School learned about obeying their parents.

Scary Time

At Sunshine Elementary Lilly and Lucky Lambkin are walking out the door with their friends, Susie Squirrel, Doolee Dog, and Ronnie Rabbit. It's been a fun day and the friends didn't want to end it by going right home.

Lilly said, "It's been such a great day. Let's skip riding the bus and just play here on the playground."

"Righto," said Susie. "The sun is shining so bright and the air feels great as I swing."

"But, we're supposed to ride the bus home right after school," said Lucky. "Won't Mom and Dad get angry with us if we don't go right home?"

"My parents are working and I just go in and watch television anyway," commented Ronnie. "Will your folks know?"

Lilly and Lucky laughed. "Not today," said Lilly. "Mom said we should just have some cookies and juice and watch television until she gets home."

"Yeah," said Lucky. "Usually we have chores to do but today we don't have to worry about that so I guess it's okay if we stay a little later."

"Well, it's too late to worry about it now," Susie laughed. "There goes the bus!"

The four friends had a great time playing on the slide, merry-go-round and the log house where they would climb the four sets of steps to the very top and jump and yell, "We can do anything, no one is here to watch us."

"Isn't this fun?" yelled Ronnie.

They were really enjoying themselves when Lucky accidentally bumped into Lilly on the slide and she yelled at him. He told her to quit being a sissy and went up the slide again.

"Ouch, that hurt and I'm not a sissy," yelled Lilly as she walked to the edge of the playground.

Now Lilly wasn't really hurt very badly, but her feelings were hurt because both Susie and Doolee kept right on playing with Lucky and ignored Lilly.

"I'll show them," she muttered and she went out to the sidewalk and started walking home. About a block away from the school yard, a car pulled up beside her and this kindly looking woman opened the door and said, "Hello, Lilly. Do you want a ride home?"

Lilly knew her parents didn't want her to ever accept a ride from anyone and she didn't recognize the woman, but she thought it would be okay because the woman called Lilly by name.

"Sure," Lilly said and climbed into the car and off they went.

Meanwhile, back at the playground, Lucky looked up just in time to see Lilly get in a car which he did not recognize. He went running after the car because he was suddenly very scared.

Susie and Doolee looked up and saw the same thing. They went running, too. "Who took Lilly in their car?" yelled Susie to Lucky as they all ran down the street chasing after the car.

"I don't know," screamed Lucky. "What'll we do?"

The car disappeared and the three stopped and looked at each other.

(The teacher stops reading and asks the following questions.)

1. How did the children get into this problem? (They stayed at the school and played.)
2. Why did they get into this problem? (They disobeyed their parents.)
3. What should they have done? (They should have gone home on the bus.)
4. What should they do now? (Have students brainstorm solutions.)

26

5.   What do you suppose is happening to Lilly? (Have students brainstorm possibilities.)

(The teacher says, "Let's find out what is going to happen next."
The teacher continues reading.)

The three worried friends thought about what to do.

"It's all my fault," Lucky cried as tears started to fall down his cheeks. "Poor Lilly. What am I going to do? Mom and Dad will never forgive me for losing Lilly. What are we going to do?"

"There, there, Lucky," said Doolee. "It'll be okay. We can call the police and get help for Lilly. Did any of you guys get the license number?"

"Oh, " said Lucky. "I was so worried about Lilly I didn't get it but I know the car was a black Ford."

"Let's not wait around," said Susie. "Doolee's right. Let's hurry to the Sunshine Grocery Store down the street and call the police."

At the grocery store, the children asked to use the phone and after they explained the problem to the clerk, the clerk called 911 for the children and the police said they would be right there.

In minutes, the police car arrived and picked up the children. As they headed home, the youngsters told the police that they had disobeyed their parents and stayed at school to play but Lilly got angry and left by herself. Lucky told them she got into a black Ford.

As the police car drove into the Lambkin's driveway, Lucky said, "There's Mom and Dad's car. Lilly's gone and I'm in real trouble."

The children jumped out of the car and ran to the door with the police right behind them. The door opened and Mrs. Lambkin stood there as Lucky started crying, "Mom, I'm so sorry. Lilly's gone and it's my fault."

"Why no she isn't. She's right here and I've been scolding her for missing the bus and accepting a ride home without my permission."

Officer Bull said, "You mean the little lamb is home and okay?"

"Yes," said Mrs. Lambkin. "A friend of mine picked her up and brought her home. But Lilly was wrong to get in the car with anyone. Thank you for helping the children."

Officer Bull said, "We care about children and we were worried about Lilly. I'm glad everything turned out good this time." The police officer left.

Just then Lilly came into the room and Lucky gave her a hug and said, "I was so worried."

"I'll just bet your parents are worried about you," Mrs. Lambkin told Doolee and Susie. "I'll call them and take you home."

The four friends looked at each other and Susie said, "You know, my Mom always says we should learn a lesson when we make a mistake. I think we learned that we should obey our parents."

"Yeah," agreed Doolee. "We shouldn't have stayed at school and played."

"And I shouldn't have gotten into a car with anyone because it's dangerous."

"Boy, we'll know not to do that again," said Lucky and all agreed, "Yeah!"

⚠ Discussion Questions

1. What did happen to Lilly? (Mom's friend took her home.)

2. What did Lucky, Susie, and Doolee decide to do when Lilly got into the car? (Call the police.)

3. What do you think about that decision? (Children will think it's a good decision.)

4. What lesson did the four friends learn? (To obey their parents.)

5. Have any of you ever gotten into danger when you didn't obey your parents?

🏃 Activities

1. Draw and color a picture of a time you got into trouble because you didn't obey your parents.

2. Describe what happened in your picture to the class.

🙎 Role Play

What would you do if . . .

1. Jimmy is trying to talk you into going down to the river to skip rocks. Your mom and dad do not allow you to go by the river without an adult.

2. Sally wants you to stay at the park and play after dark. Rule: You are to be home before dark.

3. Jill wants you to take a short cut home. Mom says never take a short cut home.

4. Jon wants to drink grape juice in your living room. Rule: No drinks in the living room.

5. You have homework but your friend, Dan, wants you to play a new computer game. Rule: Homework must be done before you play.

6. You and your sister want to eat the cookies mom baked. She left a note saying that you were not to eat the cookies until after dinner.

7. You and Mike want to ride bikes right after school. Rule: The dog must be fed and watered when you get home from school.

8. Your brother is teasing you about liking a boy at school and you are so angry you want to punch him. Rule: No hitting or other unwanted touching.

9. Ben is over visiting and the two of you are considering watching an R-rated movie on television. Rule: The children are not allowed to watch R-rated movies.

10. You and Joan want to play with your brother's new computer and he is not home to give permission. Rule: Ask permission before using other family members' things.

✓ Lesson 8: Honesty

Honesty — Honesty is when you tell the truth.

Being honest at all times is very important if we want to have the trust and respect of others. Even if we make a mistake and are scared to admit it, others will be proud of us for telling the truth. If we have a habit of lying about things and people find out we lie, then they will not believe us when we tell the truth. When we hear the saying "honesty is the best policy" it is essential that we know this is right and always tell the truth.

Directions: Read and discuss the introduction. Ask students what they have been learning about responsibility this year and have them give some example of responsible behavior. (Do chores, work at school, obey parents, take care of your feelings, cooperate in a group, and admit if you make a mistake.) Ask what they think responsibility has to do with honesty. (It is always our responsibility to be honest and tell the truth.) If using puppets, chose students to represent the characters and have them stand where they can be seen by all class members. After giving out the puppets, explain that when they hear their character (puppet) talk in the story, they are to raise the puppet so the other students can see which character is talking. Tell the students that the story today is about the Sunshine School first graders and what they learn about honesty. Tell them to listen carefully so they will be able to discuss the story and what it has to do with honesty.

Show and Tell

It is the big day — Show-and-Tell Day — and all the students in both Mrs. Owl's and Miss Lion's classrooms at Sunshine Elementary are excited. Everyone has brought their favorite thing for show and tell. Lucky Lambkin brought his Ninja, Doolee Dog brought his Spiderman. Cherry Chicken brought the poem she wrote, Kathy Kat brought her newest Barbie doll, the bride one, Susie Squirrel brought her favorite earrings that she just received for her birthday, and Mrs. Owl brought a lovely antique vase. Miss Lion brought her stuffed monkey which reminded her of the live monkeys in her homeland of Africa.

All the children were eager for show-and-tell time which in Miss Lion's room happened after lunch. Lucky was showing off his Ninja and Doolee had fun with his Spiderman until Miss Lion told them all to put their items away until after lunch.

"Aw, gee," said Lucky. "My Ninja is the best."

"Nope," said Doolee. "Spiderman takes on all evil people and wins."

"Well, my Barbie is the coolest," said Kathy. "She's getting ready to marry Ken and she is so beautiful."

"She is gorgeous," agreed Cherry.

"Yes," agreed Lucky. "She's sure pretty. Maybe she could marry my Ninja."

As students finished their printing exercise, Miss Lion said, "It's time for lunch. Line up and get your money ready. If you have lunch tickets, get them out before you leave the room."

The students all set their show-and-tell items on their desks and got in line.

"I can hardly wait for lunch to be over," said Kathy. "I just wish someone would have brought Ken, then we could have a real marriage."

"Oh, come on," said Susie. "Let's go find Lilly and see what she brought. Then let's play tag."

Off they all went to the lunch room to eat first then go outside to play.

Lucky glanced at Barbie as he went out and poked Doolee. "Let's sneak back in and have an early wedding between my Ninja and Barbie."

Doolee laughed and said, "Why not my Spiderman? " as they went out the door.

Lunch hour was about over when Doolee and Lucky sneaked back into the room. Miss Lion wasn't in the room yet.

"Okay, let's hurry. Miss Lion will be back soon," said Lucky as he and Doolee grabbed their toys and took them to Kathy's desk.

"I still think Spiderman should marry Barbie," said Doolee and he grabbed Barbie.

"No way," said Lucky. "It was my idea. Spiderman can be the marrying guy."

"Well, okay," agreed Doolee.

Lucky grabbed both Barbie and Ninja and jumped them up and down toward each other as Doolee flew Spiderman over to the desk. Lucky started laughing because the Ninja and Barbie looked so funny and he accidentally dropped Barbie on the floor. When he picked her up, the leg didn't come with the doll.

"Oh, no, you broke her leg off," said Doolee.

"Geez, you're right. Am I ever going to be in trouble," said Lucky. "Let's get out of here."

Lucky quickly propped Barbie back on Kathy's desk with her leg under her and the two boys ran back out to the playground.

(The teacher stops the story now and asks students what would be the honest thing for Lucky and Doolee to do. What do you think they will do? Teacher leads discussion about how hard it would be for Doolee and Lucky to tell Kathy and the rest of the students what happened. Then she says, "Let's read the rest of the story and find out what they do.")

Everyone came back into the classroom excited about Show and Tell. They all picked up their items and Kathy let out a cry, "My Barbie lost her leg. Look, it's broken. What could have happened? She was okay when I went out to lunch."

Miss Lion, who is a bright teacher, looked around at the class and said, "I think something happened during lunch recess. Does anybody know what could have happened?"

"Someone came back into the room and played with Kathy's Barbie," volunteered Susie. "They broke her."

Several of the students agreed.

"Do you really think that happened?" said Miss Lion. "Remember how we have been talking about responsibility and how we all need to be honest and take responsibility for what we do, even if it is an accident. I am sorry, Kathy, that your Barbie is broken, but I can't believe that anyone would have done it on purpose so perhaps it was an accident. Does anyone want to show that they are honest, responsible people and tell us just what did happen?"

Doolee poked Lucky and Lucky whispered, "Do I have to tell?"

Doolee whispered back, "I'll stand up with you since it was partly my fault, too."

Miss Lion noticed the two boys whispering and said, "Do you boys have something to tell us?"

With a sad look on his face, Lucky stood up and said, "I did it."

"What did you do?" asked Miss Lion.

"I was partly responsible, too," said Doolee.

"All right, let's hear the full story," said Miss Lion.

The two boys told how they decided to have Barbie marry Ninja and how Lucky accidentally dropped Barbie.

"I'm so sorry," Lucky said as he looked right at Kathy.

"What am I going to do?" said Kathy as tears came to her little cat eyes.

"Yes, that is a problem," agreed Miss Lion. "What can be done now? Do you have any ideas, Lucky and Doolee?"

"My uncle, Rocky Ram, is really good with toys. He fixes all kinds of toys and fixed Lilly's doll once. I'll bet he could fix Barbie in his workshop," said Lucky. "Miss Lion, could I arrange for Kathy to come to my uncle's shop to get Barbie fixed?"

"Lucky, I'm proud of you for being honest and coming up with a way to fix your mistake and I'm proud of Doolee for taking responsibility too. Kathy, is Lucky's solution all right with you?"

"Yes," said Kathy as she wiped the last of her tears away.

⚠ Discussion Questions

1. What did Lucky and Doolee do that caused a problem? (Sneaked into the classroom and broke Kathy's Barbie.)

2. How did Kathy feel about her broken Barbie doll? (She was upset and cried.)

3. What did the teacher say that helped Doolee and Lucky decide what they had to do? (Told the class that it was their responsibility to be honest.)

4. What did Doolee and Lucky do when the broken doll was discovered? (They admitted their mistake.)

5. Did Doolee and Lucky do what you thought they would do? (Various)

6. Do you think it was hard for them to be honest and tell the truth? (Various)

7. Have you ever told a lie when you should have been honest? What happened? (Call on several students to answer this.)

8. Tell about a time when someone was not honest with you? Do you trust them anymore?

🏃 Activities

1. Draw a picture of a time you were honest about something that happened.

2. Have the students play the game "true or false." The teacher chooses one student to be IT and that person asks another student a question. (Some questions to be asked: What is your favorite food? Who is your best friend? Do you like to play this game?) That student answers the question but first tells the teacher who writes down whether the answer is true or false. Everyone votes (possibly by raising their hands) on whether the answer is true or false. The teacher then tells the group which it is. A new person is chosen to play IT.

3. Have students discuss why people sometimes tell lies (they don't want others to find out what they did, etc.) and what problems can result from lying (they often get into more trouble and have to lie again to cover up for the first lie, like the lie, "I didn't break that," which could lead to the lie, "Jerry must have broken it.").

♐ Role Play

How would you practice honesty if . . .

1. Mom saw the purple stain on the carpet and asked you and your sister what happened.

2. The teacher asked if you copied Fred's paper.

3. You and Bob found a five-dollar bill laying on the floor at Bob's house.

4. You and Jon accidentally broke your brother's toy.

5. Mom left out cookies and asked you and your sister what happened to all of them.

6. Your teacher sent a note home for you to give to your mom.

7. You borrowed your friend's paints and forgot to return them and he wants them back.

8. You took some of your sister's Christmas candy and she wants to know where it went.

9. You were wearing your brother's jacket and now you can't find it and he wants it.

10. You broke Bob's pencil and he wants to know where it is.

✓ Lesson 9: Self-Control

> Self-Control – Self-control is to have power over or be
> able to discipline our thoughts, feelings, or behavior.
> To use self-control we must stop and think before we act.

Having self-control is to be in charge of our behavior. Even if something exciting and fun comes up, we must stop and think before we act. We need to think about the possible consequences of our behavior and use self-control to avoid hurting others. We must control our behavior so that we finish a task that is our responsibility. We also must use self-control in other ways. If we get angry and want to hit someone, we must use self-control. If somebody has some thing we want, we must use self-control and not grab it. If we see some money laying around, we must use self-control and not just take it but ask whose it is. It is the responsibility of each of us to practice self-control so that we grow up to be someone who can be trusted.

Directions: Read and discuss the introduction. Review what students have been learning about practicing responsible behavior. (Being responsible is to be held accountable.) Ask students what they think responsibility has to do with self-control. (It is the responsibility of each of us to practice self-control and be in charge of our behavior.) If using puppets, select students to represent the characters in the story and have them raise their puppets when they hear the teacher say the name of their character in the story. Tell the students to listen to the story so they will be able to discuss what Susie Squirrel learns about self-control.

The Brownie Meeting

Susie Squirrel was on her way to the Brownie meeting after school. She was thinking about the holiday decorations they were going to make at the meeting at Lilly Lambkin's house. She knew they wouldn't start the meeting until she got there since she was the one who had promised to bring the egg cartons they were going to use to make the decorations. She felt real proud since she had taken care of the six cartons her mother had given her that morning.

As she was scurrying along, Ted Turkey jumped out from behind a tree and said, "Boo." Susie jumped back and almost fell on her sack of egg cartons. She looked at Ted and said angrily, "Why did you scare me? I almost fell down."

Ted laughed his funny gobble-gobble laugh and said, "I'm just so happy because I get to go to Minnie's house and play computer games. But the very best thing is we are going to get to have a special treat. Minnie asked me to invite you."

Susie said importantly, "I can't come. I have to go to my Brownie meeting because I have the egg cartons."

"Egg cartons, what do you need those for at a silly old Brownie meeting?" asked Ted.

"We are going to make decorations for the holiday and we are going to use my egg cartons," said Susie. "So, I can't come. Tell Minnie I would love to come play but I can't."

"Oh, well, that just means more chocolate chip ice cream for me," grinned Ted. "We thought of you because we know how much you like chocolate chip ice cream." And he turned to go. "Of course, if you want to go make dumb decorations, that's okay. I'll be glad to eat your share of chocolate chip ice cream."

Susie sighed and Ted heard her so he just stood and looked at her. "Oh, I really love chocolate chip ice cream. It is the most yummy treat," Susie said with another big sigh.

"Aw, come on. You can go to that old Brownie meeting a little late. Nobody will care," said Ted. "And Minnie's big sister is babysitting this time and she said Minnie could have two friends come eat ice cream then play computer games."

"Okay," Susie said. "Let's go." Without a thought about the consequences of her actions, the two of them skipped off to Minnie's house.

Minnie was so glad to see them and her sister, Mabell Moo, greeted them laughingly with a big "Moo Hello."

Minnie said, "Can we have the ice cream now? We're hungry."

"Right on," said Mabell as she started dishing up the chocolate chip ice cream.

"That's my very favorite ice cream," said Susie as her mouth watered and she wiggled in delight.

The three friends had some soda pop along with their ice cream and Susie enjoyed every single bite. In fact, she mushed it around at the last, stirring it so that it was creamy and she scraped her dish to get every last bit then smacked her lips. "That was so-o-o good, Minnie," she told her friend.

Then the three went into Minnie's bedroom to play on the computer. Susie had forgotten all about the Brownies and her responsibility to get the egg cartons to the meeting. Would Susie ever think of the Brownies who depended upon her?

Susie didn't! She kept playing and playing and it was so much fun, until one game where the friends had to decide whether or not to click on the Brown Bear to go to a fun meeting or whether to click on a party with cookies and ice cream.

Suddenly, Susie stood up and yelled, "Oh, no, I forgot about the Brownies. I have to go now. They are depending on me for the egg cartons." With that she ran out of the house, grabbing her paper sack full of the six egg cartons. "I hope I'm not too late," she said as she ran all the way to Lilly's house.

She slowed down to a walk as she went up the steps and her package of egg cartons was dragging behind her. Susie knew she had done wrong and she didn't know how to explain that she had gone to eat chocolate chip ice cream at Minnie's house, when everyone was depending on her. Then she noticed her mother's car in the driveway and knew she was in real trouble.

She thought of just running home and pretending she was sick, but decided she couldn't run away. She sighed as she rang the doorbell.

Lucky answered the door. "Boy, are you in trouble!" he said. "Hey, mom, Susie's finally here."

Both Lucky and Lilly's mom and Susie's mother came rushing to the doorway where Susie still stood looking scared.

"Honey, where have you been?" said Mrs. Squirrel. "I was so worried I almost called the police."

Susie felt even worse. "I'm so sorry."

Lucky said, "Well, you should be. None of us got to make any decorations because we were counting on you. Look, over there, Lilly is crying."

"I'm so sorry," Susie said again.

"What happened to you?" asked her mother.

Again Susie thought of saying that she got sick or something, but she knew she had to tell the truth. "I stopped to play computer games and eat chocolate chip ice cream at Minnie Moo's."

Both mothers just looked at her and Lucky walked away in anger.

Lilly was still crying, but through her sobs said, "You ruined our whole meeting. We were depending on you. We didn't get to make the decorations for our moms. And I wanted to make one really bad. I'm really hurt because you let all of us down. We all work together and help each other because we're Brownies."

Susie said, "I know. I feel terrible. I should have come to the meeting," and Susie started crying. "What can I do to make it up so the Brownies will like me again?"

Mrs. Lambkin said, "The Brownies will always like you but you did disappoint them a lot. Maybe you can think of something to show them that you can have self-control and still be trusted."

Everyone waited while Susie thought, then through her tears, she said, "Mom, can I have the Brownies come to our house tomorrow? I will call them all and invite them and we will make the decorations then. I will use my allowance to pay for chocolate chip ice cream and soda pop for the snack for everybody. I would like Mrs. Lambkin to come, too. Would you let me do that, Mom?"

Mrs. Squirrel smiled and hugged her little squirrel girl, "Honey, that will be fine. That is a good way to show you really can be responsible. You can give me the money you have saved in your piggy bank and I will get the chocolate chip ice cream on the way home from work tomorrow. Mrs. Lambkin, is that all right with you?"

Mrs. Lambkin said, "That's fine. It should help make up for the disappointment the Brownies felt today. What do you think, Lilly?"

Lilly hopped off the chair and came up to Susie. "Well, the chocolate chip ice cream snack will help make up for today," she said because chocolate chip ice cream was her very favorite ice cream, too.

⚠? Discussion Questions

1. What is self-control? (To have control of your behavior and emotions.)
2. What were the Brownies going to do at their meeting? (Make holiday decorations.)
3. What was Susie Squirrel supposed to bring to the meeting? (Six egg cartons)
4. Why didn't Susie go to the meeting? (She wanted to eat her favorite ice cream and play computer games.)
5. How did Susie's lack of self-control hurt others? (The Brownies didn't get to make their decorations. Lucky was angry and Lilly was crying and both mothers were worried.)
6. How did Susie show that she knew she had not practiced self-control? (She cried and came up with an idea to make up for her lack of responsibility.)
7. Tell about a time that you didn't use self-control? What was the result?

🏃 Activities

1. Draw a picture showing a time when you showed self-control. Color it.
2. Pick a color that shows how one of the characters felt and draw that character using that color. Share the picture "feeling" with the class or other students.
3. Tell what your favorite ice cream flavor is and tell why it is your favorite. Tell whether or not you would miss a meeting to have some. Tell about the last time you had your favorite ice cream.

Role Play

How would you practice self-control if . . .

1. Jill wants you to go eat ice cream instead of going to a meeting.
2. Bob has a toy that you want.
3. You want to buy some gum and there is a quarter laying on your mom's table.
4. Your friend Diane left her sweater at your house and you think of keeping it.
5. Joe wants to fight with you.
6. Linda has a color crayon you want.
7. Your mom left cupcakes out to cool and you know they are for after dinner.
8. Betsy is in a swing and you want to push her out.
9. Ron and you are playing a board game and you want to move a game piece when he's not looking.
10. You are watching your sister and Stacy wants you to go to the park.

☑ Lesson 10: Anger Management

Anger Management — Anger is the feeling we have toward something or someone that hurts, opposes, offends, or annoys. Management is the ability to handle or control our anger.

It's okay to feel angry but we all must learn to manage our behavior when we are angry so no one gets hurt. Learning to handle our anger is sometimes hard because sometimes we have our feelings hurt or we are actually hurt physically. Perhaps you once had someone hit you and it hurt so you hit them back and they hit you back. This goes on and on until it is a real fight. Then someone cries or somebody else must stop the fight. We can learn to manage our behavior when we are angry by learning ways to manage our anger. It is important for us to learn ways to calm down when we're angry so we can think clearly and behave appropriately. It is our responsibility to manage our own anger because no one else can do it for us.

Directions: Read and discuss the introduction. Include the steps to anger management:

1. Take three deep breaths and count to 10.
2. Talk about why you are angry.
3. If possible, do an activity that makes you feel calm (a favorite hobby, play a game, ride your bicycle, swing, read).

Discuss how it's our responsibility to know these steps and practice them so we can have the feeling of anger without hurting anyone. Stress that all feelings are okay but it is **never** okay to hurt anyone.

If using puppets, select four students to represent the characters in the story and have them raise their puppets when they hear the teacher say the name of their character. Tell the students to listen to the story so they can tell how Lucky Lambkin learned to handle his anger.

Anger Management

Lilly Lambkin came home right after school and brought her friend, Cherry Chicken, home to play until Cherry's mother got home. Lilly's mother was gone but she had left a big plate of cookies and a note that said, "Help yourself to the milk and cookies."

"It is fun to have you here, today," Lilly said, "especially since Lucky had to stay after school to practice soccer."

"M-m-m, yeah," said Cherry with her mouth full of peanut butter cookie.

"What do you want to do?" asked Lilly.

"I don't know. What do you want to do?" said Cherry.

"I know," Lilly laughed in delight. "Let's go to Lucky's room and play with his new electric train set. That's lots of fun."

"Do you know how to work it?" asked Cherry.

"Sure," said Lilly even though she had only seen her uncle Rocky Ram show Lucky how to run the train set when Lucky got it for his birthday a few weeks ago. Lucky hadn't had much time to teach Lilly how to run it so he told her she absolutely could not go into his room and play with it until he taught her how to run it.

Lilly thought she knew what to do. What could be so hard? So, the two girls went upstairs and into Lucky's room where the train was set up and ready to roll.

"Wow," said Cherry. "This looks like fun. What do we do first?"

"Easy," said Lilly. "We just turn it on." She flipped the switch and was a bit relieved that the control light went on.

Working the engine wasn't too hard and the girls soon had it just ripping around the track. It was lots of fun to watch. Then Lilly said, "Let's hook all the cars up and see how fast we can make it go."

"Okay," agreed Cherry. Both girls got busy and hooked up all the cars and Lilly started the train around the track. It went slowly past the little depot where all the little people figures were standing and she got it going faster as it went around the second curve. Then it was really sailing and both girls started laughing. Lilly thought, I wonder what would happen if I put the whole thing in reverse. Then she immediately pushed the lever in reverse position.

Wow, things did happen. The train didn't just grind to a stop, it slammed all the cars into each other and threw them off the track.

Lilly was horrified and quickly rammed the lever the other way and the two girls heard a grinding noise and the motor died.

The two girls tried to get the cars and engine back on the track but some of the wheels were bent and even though Lilly kept trying, the electricity just didn't seem to be making the engine go again.

"It's broke," cried Cherry.

"I know. What will I do?" said Lilly.

Cherry said, "I'd like to help but my mom is expecting me home right now. So, I've got to go. I'll call you later." And off she ran.

First Grade Lesson 10: ANGER MANAGEMENT

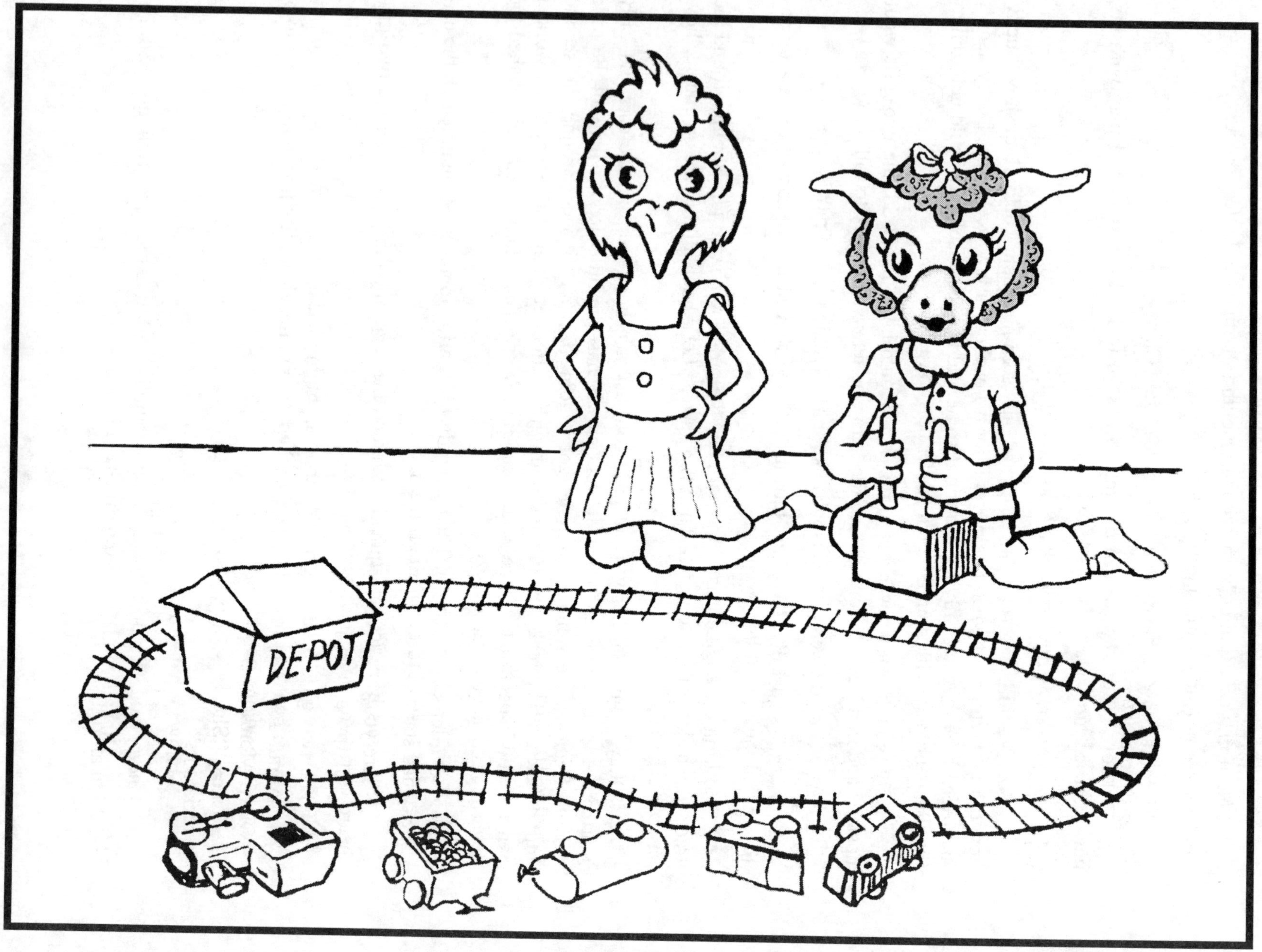

"Geez, I'm in trouble," Lilly said as she hurried out of Lucky's room because she heard her mother and Lucky coming in the door.

Instead of running right down and telling what she did, Lilly went to her room and just answered her mother's call by, "Yeah, mom. I'm home. I'm upstairs in my room."

Lucky ran up to his room to change from his soccer clothes and Lilly cringed as she hear him yell, "Who's ruined my train?" Then he came pounding on her door. "Lilly, what did you do to my new train?"

"Nothin'," said Lilly but she checked to be sure her door was locked.

Lucky kept pounding and screaming, "You're going to get it when I get my hands on you, you wrecker. You weren't supposed to play with my special birthday train. You wrecked it and Uncle Rocky gave it to me. You are an awful person and when I get you, you're going to be sorry."

Lilly was hiding her head under her pillow when she heard her mother come up the stairs saying, "What on earth is going on up here? What is your problem, Lucky?"

"Come in and see what Lilly did to my brand new train set Uncle Rocky gave me," said Lucky as he pulled his mother into his bedroom.

"Oh," said Mrs. Lambkin as she tried to turn the engine on and they only heard a grinding, grating noise. "I think you had better wait until your dad comes home and looks at it."

"I hate Lilly. I hate Lilly. Why did she break it?" Lucky cried to his mother.

"Lucky, you need to calm down and handle your anger. Take three deep breaths and count to 10. Then we'll talk."

"I don't want to," said Lucky. "I hate her. She broke my train."

"Three deep breaths," repeated his mom. "Let's do it together . . . one . . . two . . . three. Now, let's count to 10." Together they counted to 10. By the time they got to five, Lucky had started to calm down, and by the time they got to 10 he looked much calmer.

"Are you okay?" she asked. "Why don't you go ride your bike around the block a couple of times and come back for your cookies and milk. Then we'll talk about what happened."

About 15 minutes later Lucky came into the house and ate his cookies and milk. "Okay, Mom. What's going to happen to Lilly and how can we get my train set fixed?" he asked. "She did go into my room and play with my train set without permission and wrecked it."

"First of all, I want to tell you how proud I am of you that you managed your anger and didn't hit Lilly," his mother said. "Let's call Lilly down and see what she has to say. Are you all right with that?"

"Sure," said Lucky. "I promise that I won't hit her because I'm not so angry any more. Besides, I want to know why she played with it."

After Lilly came down, with her head hanging very low, she wiped her eyes and said, "Lucky, I'm so sorry I broke your train. Cherry came over and we decided to play with it and I was showing off. I'm sorry. What can I do to make up for it?"

"See," said Mrs. Lambkin, "Lilly made a mistake but she does take responsibility and wants to make things right. Yes, she was wrong to come into your room and play with your new train, but do you think she really tried to break it on purpose?"

"No, I don't think she meant to do it," said Lucky. "But, she did wreck it. What am I going to do?"

"Well, if your dad can't fix it, we'll call Uncle Rocky and see if he can because he is great with electric trains," said Mrs. Lambkin. "But if there are any parts that need to be replaced, I think someone in this room . . ."

Mrs. Lambkin didn't finish her statement because Lilly cried out, "I will use my allowance to get any part you need, Lucky. I am so sorry. Will you ever forgive me?"

"Sure," said Lucky, secretly glad he had learned to manager his anger and not hit Lilly. After all, she was his sister and not so bad, for a girl.

Lilly looked at her brother fondly, glad he was her brother because he really wasn't too awful, for a boy.

⚠ Discussion Questions

1. What is anger management? (To be able to control your behavior when feeling angry.)
2. What caused Lucky to lose his temper? (He found his train wrecked.)
3. Who was responsible for wrecking his new train set? (Lilly actually caused it to wreck but Cherry was also responsible.)
4. Did Cherry take any responsibility? (No, she left.)
5. Did Lilly take any responsibility? (Yes, she did finally.)
6. How did Mom teach Lucky to control his anger? (She had him take three deep breaths and count to 10 then go ride his bike. Later she had him talk about it.)
7. What are some other things Lucky could have done to help control his anger? (Any kind of activity or hobby would help and talking about it also is important.)
8. How do you manage your anger?
9. Tell of a time when you got angry and did or did not control your anger. Tell what you did or should have done.

🜋 Activities

1. Draw a picture showing a time when you managed your anger.
2. Pick a color that shows how Lucky felt and draw him using just that color. Share the picture with the class or other students.

🜋 Role Play

Direct students to practice steps to managing anger in the following role plays.

1. Take three deep breaths and count to 10.
2. Talk about why you are angry.
3. If possible, do an activity that makes you feel calm (a favorite hobby, play a game, ride your bicycle, swing, read).

How would you practice anger management if . . .

1. A friend accidentally hits you with her feet as you go down the slide.
2. Your sister breaks your toy.
3. Your brother walks into the room and turns the television off in the middle of your program.
4. A friend eats your most favorite cupcake while you are getting a drink of water.
5. You are playing football and your friend grabs you and tears your favorite shirt.
6. A friend accidentally breaks the arm off your Barbie.
7. You took the basketball out at recess and a classmate takes it from you and won't give it back.
8. Playing baseball, you slid to home base and you were called out when you thought you were safe.
9. A friend called you a name when you were playing at recess.
10. Mom and Dad promised to take you to the movies but they couldn't do it.

☑ Lesson 11: Listening

> Listening — Listening is paying attention to what someone is saying and actually hearing what they say so we can respond to their comment.

It is our responsibility to be good listeners. The three keys to being a good listener are:

- Look at the person talking.
- Do not interrupt.
- Show you are listening by saying "wow" or "great" or asking questions or making comments about what the speaker said.

Some of the reasons why we all need to be good listeners include: we can discover things about others, we can show our friends we care about them and their activities and by listening we show them the same respect as we want them to give us. Listening also holds the key to learning. Being a good listener helps us learn from others, particularly our teachers. Learning to be a good listener will help us to be a good student.

Directions: Review what students have been learning about responsibility and tell them that it is our responsibility to be good listeners. Write on the board and teach the keys to good listening that are listed above. After some discussion, review the following questions:

1. What have you learned a person should do to show he is a good listener? (Look at the person speaking, listen to what the speaker is saying, don't interrupt, and give responses that show you are listening.)

2. How do you learn to be a good listener? (Practice the three keys to being a good listener.)

3. Why does being a good listener mean you are showing responsibility? (Because it shows you care about others and what they are saying, because you want to learn, etc.)

Practicing Listening Skills

Teacher: We have said we know some of the things it takes to be a good listener, now I want you to watch a skit and see if you think I am being a good listener. The teacher then asks one student to come up and tell about a vacation they went on recently. As the student talks, the teacher demonstrates bad listening in an exaggerated manner by doing some of the following: yawns, fiddles with her pencil, scratches her head, looks out the window, taps her foot and interrupts, or other distracting behaviors.

Then the teacher asks the students whether or not she was a good listener. They should say "No." Then she asks what she did wrong? (They will name the behaviors that show she was a bad listener.) Teacher asks the student how he felt when it was obvious that she was not listening.

Teacher: Watch the skit we are going to do now and see if I do better this time. Then she asks the same student to again talk about a vacation or a family outing. As the student talks, the teacher listens intently, makes eye contact, nods her head, makes approving comments, leans forward to hear better, does not interrupt, and may even ask a question that shows she has been listening.

She asks the students what she did differently this time? (They should respond with some of her various actions.) Teacher asks the student how they felt when it was obvious that she was listening this time.

The teacher again talks about the keys to being a good listener.

- Look at the person talking.
- Do not interrupt.
- Show interest by saying things like "wow," "really," or just nod.

Teacher: We are going to do an activity where we will practice keys to good listening. Teacher has two students come up to listen to another student talk about a vacation, a fun time, a book they have just read, or something funny that happened in class or at home. The rest of the class watches and then discusses and names which of the three keys the listeners used to show they were good listeners. Continue this exercise until all students have had a chance to be in front of the class.

⚠ Discussion Questions

1. Did anyone have any problems staying on task and listening by using the three keys? (various)

2. What are the three keys to good listening? (Make eye contact with the person. Let them finish their story. Show interest by saying things like "wow," "really," or just nod.)

3. Why is it our responsibility to be a good listener? (Show respect and learn, etc.)

4. Tell about a time when someone did not listen to you. Tell how you felt.

5. Tell about a time when someone listened to you and showed they were really interested in what you were saying. Tell how you felt.

Ⅺ Activities

1.   Have the students draw and color pictures showing each of the three listening keys. Option: Share with class and post on classroom walls.

2.   Have students choose one of the following options: draw a picture showing how you might feel when someone *does not* listen to you or draw a picture showing how you might feel when someone *does* listen to you.

☑ Lesson 12: Listening Skit

> Listening — Listening is paying attention to what
> someone is saying and actually hearing what they say
> so we can respond to their comment.

It is our responsibility to be a good listener. The three keys to being a good listener are:

- Look at the person talking.

- Do not interrupt.

- Show you are listening by saying "wow" or "great" or asking questions or making comments about what the speaker said.

Some of the reasons why we all need to be good listeners include learning things from others but only if we hear them, we can show our friends we care about them and their activities. Also, we want others to listen to us so we must show them the same respect as we want them to give us.

Directions: Read and discuss the introduction. Review what students have learned about responsibility and ask them to name some behaviors that they have learned that show responsibility. Then ask students what responsibility has to do with listening. (It is our responsibility to show that we're a good friend by being a good listener.) The teacher may want to make some preparation for the following skit. The teacher may have adults or older students do the skit for the younger students. (A copy of the play should be made for each of the four characters.) Tell the students to listen as Lucky Lambkin talks about his trip so they'll be able to tell which friends did or did not use good listening skills

Lucky's Trip

Teacher reads the setting: Lucky, Ronnie, Doolee, and Corky were waiting in the school yard for the school bell to ring one Monday morning.

Lucky:	Hey, you guys, guess what? I had the most terrific weekend with my grandpa. We went fishing and . . .
Doolee (interrupts):	Yeh, I went fishing with my gramps last summer and we had a great week. We went fishing every day.
Ronnie:	Lucky, where did you go and how many fish did you catch?

Lucky:	It was really fun! We climbed way up in the mountains and my grandpa and I made our way to this huge lake where I caught just scads of fish. It was so much fun because . . .
Doolee (interrupts):	My dad went with us but gramps and I snuck off one day and went out in the boat, just the two of us. We saw huge fish in the lake and I caught one this (stretched his arms out wide) big! Bet you never even saw one that big!
Lucky:	Sure, I did! My grandpa measured my biggest fish and it was . . .
Doolee (interrupts):	My fish was so big (stretches arms out again). We camped out every night and we ate our food over the campfire. My dad said, "It's good for men to camp together."
Corky:	Doolee, we heard all about your vacation last fall. We want to hear how big Lucky's fish was. Lucky, how big was your fish?
Lucky:	It was 10 inches long and it really pulled hard on my line when I tried to land him. I just about . . .
Doolee (interrupts):	Gosh, that's just like the time I almost lost my pole. If my gramps hadn't grabbed it, I would have.
Lucky:	One night we stayed up real late and heard some wolves howl. At first, I was . . .
	Doolee (interrupting): Gosh, that's like the time we saw the wild mustangs running. It sounded just like thunder in the hills.
Lucky:	Aw-w-w-w, uh uh uh, Doolee!! Come on, guys, let's go into class and I'll tell you about my fun trip later.

⚠ Discussion Questions

1. What was Lucky telling his friends about? (His weekend trip to the lake.)

2. Who was not using responsible behavior? (Doolee)

3. What was Doolee doing? (He was not being a good listener — interrupting, telling about his trip, etc.)

4. What should Doolee have done to show that he could be a good listener? (He should have been looking at Lucky, let Lucky finish his story without interrupting, and shown interest in what Lucky was saying.)

5. If Doolee wanted to tell about his trip, what should he have done? (Waited until Lucky was finished talking, then tell his story.)

6. Has there ever been a time when you were telling a story and a friend interrupted you? How did you feel?

7.   Have you ever interrupted others when they are talking? Do you always realize that you are interrupting people? How can you stop doing it?

✖ Activity

Students use the puppets to work in pairs (or groups of three or four) to make up their own skit using the three keys to good listening: Look at the person talking, let the person finish their story, show interest by saying things like "wow," "great," or "really." Let students practice then, if desired, have each group go in front of the class and perform a short skit.

☑ Lesson 13: "I" Messages

"I" Messages — "I" messages are oral or written comments used when we tell how we feel by using the word "I" instead of "You."

Using "I" messages instead of "You" messages cause others to listen to you and help them understand how you feel. "You" messages usually place blame or make others feel that you are picking on them. When a "You" message is given, the other person reacts defensively and with anger. When an "I" message is given, the other person tends to listen because they don't have to get angry, so the "I" message is heard without anger and you are more likely to get what you want. If someone takes your toy and you accuse them or grab it back, they get angry. It is better to say, "I feel sad when you take my toy because I don't have anything to play with." Since you are only telling how you feel, the other person is less likely to get angry and you are more likely to get your toy back.

Directions: Read and discuss the introduction. Review what responsible behavior means and have students give examples. (Do chores, cooperate with others, take charge of our feelings, be honest, practice self-control, and practice anger management.) Ask students what responsibility has to do with knowing how to use "I" messages. (It's our responsibility to know how to use "I" messages to cause others to listen to us and help them understand how we feel. (When they understand our feelings we are more likely to get what we want.) Then follow the format below. (Advance preparation: make two copies of the skit and have a student or adult prepare to read the skit with the teacher.)

1. Tell the students there are two ways to express our feelings: "I" messages and "You" messages.

2. Explain what "I" messages are (when the speaker tells how they feel) and explain what "You" messages are (when the speaker places the blame on "You" and accuses you of doing or saying something that causes problems, etc.).

3. Write the "I" message formula (see Appendix B, Resource Sheet 2) on the board:

    I feel _____ when _____ because _____.

4. Give examples on how "I" messages fit into the formula. (I *feel* hurt *when* you don't talk to me *because* I think you don't like me. I *feel* sad *when* you won't let me play *because* I don't have anyone to play with.)

5. Give examples of "You" messages that accuse, criticize, or blame the other person. You don't need to give many examples of "You" messages because the students already know how to use those, e.g., you are mean and you never play with me, you always take my toys.

6. Ask the students which of the two ways of expressing yourself sounds better and helps you get what you want, the "I" messages or the "You" messages. ("I" messages)

7. Tell the students you are now going to perform two skits involving Cherry Chicken and Lilly Lambkin.

8. **Emphasize** that students should listen to the first skit carefully so they will be able to tell if it is an "I" message skit or a "You" message skit.

Cherry: Lilly, you pushed me out of the swing. You are mean and selfish. You always think you can push me around on the playground. You're mean and you are never going to be my friend again and you're never going to get to eat any of my chocolate chip cookies again and you can't sit by me on the bus ever again.

Lilly: Cherry, you're always the one who keeps the swing the whole recess. You never let me have a turn in any game we play. You are selfish and you don't ever think of anyone else and you can't come to my house to play ever again.

9. Ask the students if this skit shows an "I" message or "You" message. ("You" message) How can you tell?

10. Ask the students what Cherry wants from Lilly. (Lilly to stop pushing Cherry.)

11. Will Cherry get what she wants using the accusing "You" messages? (Probably not)

Tell the students to listen to the next skit carefully so they will be able to tell if it is an "I" message or a "You" message skit.

Cherry: Lilly, I feel hurt when you push me out of the swing because it was my turn to swing. I feel angry when you push me like that because I thought you were my friend. We decided that we would take turns swinging but now I feel I can't trust you to wait for your turn.

Lilly: Cherry, I'm sorry. I forgot that we were taking turns. I want to be your friend and play with you at recess and I won't push you any more. I'll be a good friend because I like you and your chocolate chip cookies and I want to sit with you on the bus.

12. Ask the students if this skit shows an "I" message or "You" message. ("I" message) How can you tell?

13. Which one is better at expressing your feelings? ("I" message) Why?

14. Ask students which skit is more likely to get Cherry what she wants (to get Lilly to stop pushing her off the swing). ("I" message. "I" messages express feelings rather than blaming and accusing.)

🐾 Activities

1. Have students brainstorm possible problem situations. (Possible ideas: your brother always switches channels when you are watching television; your friend borrows your crayons without asking; your friend always takes the ball away from you; your friend always kicks you when you are playing soccer; your sister calls you names; your friend crowds in line; your friend pushes you down; your classmate gossips about you; your brother hits you with a ball.)

2. In pairs have students role play their situations and use "I" messages to express their feelings. Teacher will prompt students to use the "I" message formula and avoid using any "You" messages in the skits. (Teacher can tell the students that they will not practice the "You" messages because they already know how to do those.) Can be teacher directed in pairs in front of class.

3. Draw and color a situation where an "I" message would help you express your feelings.

☑ **Lesson 14: Seeing Both Sides**

> **Seeing Both Sides** — Seeing both sides of an event or discussion means being able to look at another person's point of view.

When people get into a conflict often it is because they don't understand why the other person is acting or saying something that seems to be wrong to them. They must stop and really listen to what the other person is saying. Perhaps what happened was all because of a misunderstanding. Each of us has the responsibility to look at the other person's side of the story in order to resolve a conflict or problem.

Directions: Before the lesson, the teacher will review the definition of responsibility and talk about how conflict often happens because one or both sides have different ideas about what happened. Tell the students that it is our responsibility to see the other person's side of the story. For example, it is our responsibility to help settle our own conflicts by listening to and seeing what the other person thinks caused the problem. Tell the students to listen to two stories about the same event so they can explain both sides. Ask how many have heard about the story of "The Three Little Pigs." Then ask a student to tell the story. (If no students know it, teacher reminds them of the story plot.)

Then say "Do you know the wolf wants to tell his side of the story and he says that the three little pigs have it all wrong. First, we're going to hear the little pigs' side of the story, then we'll hear the wolf's side. Listen so you can tell who you think is right or if they are both right.

One Side

Here is the story as told by the oldest little pig:

Once upon a time my two brothers and I decided it was time to go out into the world and live on our own. We went off to build our houses. My youngest brother met a man who sold straw and he thought, "Wow! Straw would make a fine house." So he bought the straw and built his house in a beautiful green meadow with a stream running by.

My second brother was hunting for a place to live and found a mountain top he liked so he looked for some place where he could find his building material. He met a man who was selling wood sticks and he thought, "Wow! Wood would make a fine house." So he bought the wood and built his house on the beautiful mountain top.

I looked and looked for just the right material to build my house and just the right place to build it so it would be fine and strong. I found the perfect spot, a beautiful hill overlooking a beautiful river. So I went hunting for the perfect building material when I met a man selling bricks. "Wow! Brick would make a fine strong house," I exclaimed. I bought the brick and built my house on the beautiful hill overlooking the beautiful river.

Meanwhile, the big, bad wolf went looking for us. We weren't at our parents' home so he wandered down the road and, lo and behold, he discovered my little brother's house. He went up to the house and knocked on the door but my little brother looked out the window and cried, "Go away. I'm not going to let you in."

The wolf was upset so he said, "Let me in or by the hair of my chinny-chin-chin, I'll huff and puff and I'll blow your house in." So he did.

But my brother ran out the back door quickly and went to our other brother's wooden stick home and said, "Hurry, let me in. The wolf is after me."

Later that day as my two brothers were eating lunch, the wolf went to the top of the beautiful mountain and found my second brother's home made of sticks.

"Ah ha," the wolf said, "they *are* here and I want to see them," so he went to the door and knocked.

My two brothers looked out the window and said, "Go away. We won't let you in."

The wolf was upset so he said, "Let me in or by the hair of my chinny-chin-chin, I'll huff and puff and I'll blow your house in." So he did.

But my two brothers ran out the back door quickly and down the mountain to the beautiful hill by the beautiful river where I had built my house of brick. "Let us in," they cried. "The wolf is after us."

Later as we were eating dinner, my brothers told me that the wolf had blown their houses down. I said, "Never fear. My house is made of brick and he will not blow it down."

Sure enough, the wolf came up to my door and knocked and when I said "Go away" the wolf got upset again. He said, "Let me in or by the hair of my chinny-chin-chin, I'll huff and puff and I'll blow your house in."

I laughed and said, "Go ahead and try," so the wolf huffed and he puffed and huffed and puffed but the house did not fall down. One of the things the silly wolf did after that was get on the roof of the house and peer down the chimney. He accidentally fell down the chimney into my pot sitting on the fire.

(At this point, teacher asks the following questions.)

1.   Whose side is being told in this story? (The little pigs.)

2.   Why do you think the wolf is after the three little pigs? (To do something mean to them.)

3.   Did the three little pigs ever ask the wolf why he wanted to see them? (No)

The teacher then says, "Perhaps the wolf was not going to do anything mean to the little pigs. Let's listen to the wolf's side of the story."

The Other Side

My name is Willy Wolf and I want to tell my side of the story. I'm tired of those three little pigs telling stories about me that aren't true and ruining my reputation. This is the real truth of what happened that day.

It was a beautiful sunny day when I decided I wanted to go play. I thought I would go ask the three little pigs to come out to play with me. They weren't home. Their mother said they decided to go out on their own and build houses. I hunted until I found the littlest pig's house of straw. I went up to the door and knocked. But he was so rude. He yelled, "Go away. I'm not going to let you in." That was really mean and it hurt my feelings. I decided to play with him anyway so I told him I was going to huff and puff and blow his house down. I had no idea that that house would fall down. It really looked pretty sturdy. But it fell down.

I felt really bad about that and figured since the little pig was gone, he must have gone to his brother's house. I decided to see if I could find it and apologize to him and maybe they both would play with me.

Pretty soon I found the second brother's house of wood on top of a beautiful mountain. I was really tired after climbing that mountain but I wanted to apologize so I knocked. Would you believe it, both pigs said, "Go away. We won't let you in." Then I got a little angry. Here I had come to apologize and I was tired and they wouldn't even let me in to rest. I said the same thing I said before about huffing and puffing the house down but, of course, I was too tired to do much huffing and puffing but I gave it a try. Who would have thought a wooden house would fall down. Well, it did, but they were gone.

Now I was really sorry so after I rested I went hunting for the big brother. I found his brick house on a beautiful hill above a beautiful river. When I knocked, would you believe it, the same thing happened. Those rude pigs yelled, "Go away" to me. Well, by this time I was furious so I huffed and puffed and huffed and puffed. But the house didn't fall down. They were really beginning to get to me so I decided to climb on the roof and look down the chimney to see if I could reason with those silly pigs.

I leaned too far and before I knew it I had fallen down the chimney and into their kettle on the fire. Man, that was hot. That did it. I didn't want to play with those rude, mean little pigs ever so I hit the door running and never looked back.

The only thing that still makes me angry is that ridiculous story they are telling about how I wanted to eat those pigs. I don't even like pork. I prefer chicken.

⚠ Discussion Questions

1. Whose side is being told in this story? (The wolf)
2. Why is the wolf going to visit the little pigs? (To play)
3. Why did the wolf blow the straw house down? (They were rude.)
4. How is the wolf's side of the story different from the story told by the three little pigs. (He told it from his point of view and other various answers.)
5. What would have happened if the pigs had asked the wolf what he wanted? (Various answers depending on point of view.)
6. Tell about a time when someone didn't understand your side of what happened.
7. Tell about a time when you didn't see the other person's side of the story.

⚒ Activities

1. Draw a line across the middle of your paper and on the top half of the paper draw the pigs' side of the story and on bottom half draw the wolf's side.
2. Tell the class about your picture.

🎭 Role Play

How can you get the other person to see your side of the story if . . .

1. You borrowed Jim's ruler and he accused you of stealing it.
2. Your brother broke your toy and you thought he did it on purpose.
3. You broke your sister's toy and she thought you did it on purpose.
4. Your mother left a note not to eat the cookies but you never saw it so you ate two cookies.
5. You accidentally hit Jimmy in the stomach with a ball and he thought you did it on purpose.
6. You stumbled and fell on Mary's desk and wrinkled her paper and she got angry.
7. You told the teacher you handed in your paper and then you found it in your desk.
8. You finished coloring your sister's picture of a witch for the local Halloween contest and she cried.
9. Your brother loaned you his sweat shirt and he was angry that you left it at school.
10. Mary was upset because you didn't play with her at recess.

✓ Lesson 15: Resolving Conflicts Peacefully

> Resolving Conflicts Peacefully — Conflicts occur when two or more people disagree. Resolving conflicts peacefully is a win-win situation, not a win-lose situation. This means everyone involved in the conflict is satisfied with the solution.

Resolving conflicts peacefully means each of us involved must take the responsibility to be cooperative and solve the problem. Each person must have a chance to be heard and tell his side of the problem while the others listen. This is not always easy because each of us generally believes that our side is the "right" one. To truly resolve a conflict, each person must stop thinking of their own "side" and try to think of the other person's "side." The five steps to problem solving can help us do this.

Directions: Read the introduction and discuss the steps to resolving a problem or conflict peacefully. (See Appendix B, Resource Sheet 3 to make student copies.)

1. If you are angry, take three deep breaths and count to 10.

2. Each person states the problem. (no interrupting, name calling, or physical contact)

3. Name some solutions. (together)

4. Decide on a solution that is fair. (win-win)

5. Do the solution.

Discuss how it's our responsibility to know these steps and practice them so we can learn to resolve conflicts peacefully. If using puppets select the students to represent the characters in the story. Tell the students to listen to the story and see how Billy Goat and Doolee Dog resolve their conflict.

Recess Time

Lucky and Lilly Lambkin and their friends all ran, scurried, hopped, jumped, and galloped out the school door when the recess bell rang. They had been looking forward to recess all afternoon because the sun was shining bright for a change and they were going to play kickball.

They all headed for the position they wanted to play. Lucky called "pitcher" and Minnie Moo yelled "batter" and Ronnie Rabbit called "first base" as he hopped toward it. Billy Goat yelled "second base" as he ran to the second-base position. Kathy Kat ran to third base. Doolee Dog ran up to be catcher and all the other friends went to field positions.

Minnie yelled, "Batter up." Lucky rolled the ball right across home plate and Minnie gave it a big, giant kick and ran as fast as she could to first base just as Cherry Chicken grabbed the ball in center field and threw it to Ronnie on first base. Minnie zipped past Ronnie and stopped at second.

It was Doolee's turn to be up to kick and as he moved to the batter's position, Lilly came in from the outfield to third base and all the others moved up.

Ronnie rolled the ball in to Doolee and it came up short. Doolee was only able to barely tap it so the ball didn't roll very far. Lucky, as catcher, picked it up and tossed it to Billy on first and Billy missed the ball. Billy was so angry that before Doolee got to first, Billy tripped him. This made Doolee angry, so he got up and pushed Billy.

The whole team gathered around the two as they were yelling at each other. Then Ronnie said, "Hey, you guys, stop yelling at each other and use the problem-solving steps our teacher taught us. Remember, you have to take three deep breaths, count to 10, and cool down before we can solve the problem."

Everybody stopped yelling and Ronnie reminded them by taking three deep breaths himself. Billy and Doolee then took three deep breaths and counted to 10.

As they remembered the steps the teacher taught them, first Doolee, then Billy told the problem as they saw it.

Doolee said, "I was running to first base, Billy tripped me."

Billy said, "Doolee pushed me down."

They looked at Ronnie and he said, "Okay, you guys. You said the problems and now you need to come up with some solutions."

(The teacher has the option to stop the story here and have her class come up with some possible solutions to the problem.)

Billy, Doolee, and several of the friends came up with possible solutions to help to resolve the conflict.

Minnie said, "I think they should just never play with each other again."

Cherry said, "Replay that part of the game again."

Lucky said, "I think they should just fight after school."

Lilly suggested, "Both of you should stop playing for today."

"Billy and Doolee should both spend the rest of the game in the field," said Ted Turkey.

Corky Colt suggested, "Billy and Doolee should fight each other now."

Ronnie looked at the two players and said, "You guys have a lot of suggestions for resolving this conflict. Are you going to choose one of the suggestions or are you going to make up your own?"

Billy looked around and said, "Gosh, I don't really want to fight Doolee. We are friends and besides fighting never really solves anything."

Doolee muttered, "Yeah, I don't want to fight you either, Billy. But I don't really want to quit playing, do you?"

"No," said Billy. "How about if we both apologize to each other and you get to be on first base. I really am sorry I got so angry and tripped you."

"Yeah, well, I'm sorry I pushed you down," said Doolee. As the two friends shook hands, everybody cheered.

Ronnie said, "Since you guys handled this peacefully, let's get on with the game."

Everybody ran to their positions and the game went on.

⚠ Discussion Questions

1. What started the conflict? (Billy tripped Doolee.)

2. What did Doolee do to Billy? (Pushed him down)

3. How did the two feel about the tripping and pushing? (angry)

4. What were the steps they used to resolve the conflict? (Took three deep breaths and counted to 10 to calm down. Each stated the problem from his point of view and said their feelings. Possible solutions were given. Doolee and Billy chose a win-win solution. They did it.)

5. Did the characters resolve the conflict the way our class suggested?

6. Does any one want to tell about a recent conflict they had and how it was resolved? Did you use the steps to resolving the conflict peacefully? If not, what happened? How could such a result be prevented next time?

🏃 Activities

1. Draw a picture about a playground conflict and how it could be resolved.

2. Draw a poster showing the steps to resolving conflicts peacefully.

🎭 Role Play

How would you use the steps to resolving conflicts peacefully if . . .

1. June kept calling Lynn names so Lynn wouldn't let June sit with her on the bus.

2. Tommy took Kevin's ball away at recess so Kevin called Tommy a name.

3. Playing soccer, Bob kept bumping into John so John tripped him.

4. Richard keeps making fun of Louis so Louis pushed him down.

5. Susie keeps tattling on Mary so Mary took Susie's notebook.

6. John kept changing the television channel so his sister, Toni, pulled the plug on the television.

7. Betty took too much time in the bathroom in the mornings, so Liz locked her out of their bedroom.

8. Richie hit Tom in the stomach with a ball; Tom picked it up and hit Richie on the head with it.

9. Debbie keeps cutting in front of Renee in the lunch line so Renee called Debbie a name.

10. Vernon was drinking water at the drinking fountain when Jimmy pushed his head into the faucet and Vernon slugged Jimmy.

☑ Lesson 16: Friendship

> Friendship – Friendship is when two or more people know and like each other enough to want to spend time together enjoying each other's company.

It is our responsibility to learn how to be a good friend. We need to understand that the things we want in a friend are also the same things others want in a friend. If we want others to be friends with us, we need to practice friendly behavior ourselves. A good friend is caring, fair, helpful, honest, kind, and fun. A good friend is also willing to share and is a good sport. When you are sad, a good friend will listen to you and help you feel better. When you want to play games, a good friend will play fair, cheer you on, and never cheat. A good friend will share their candy with you. A good friend is fun. All these things are keys to being a good friend and everyone needs to practice friendly behavior.

Directions: Ask students why it is important to have friends (everyone needs someone to play with, talk to, or just be with). Ask what responsibility has to do with being a good friend. (It is our responsibility to know what to do to be a good friend and if you trust others like a friend, they will return the treatment.) Discuss with the students some things that children do that make them good friends (share candy, play games, give compliments, have fun, play fair, are honest, help you with reading). Then discuss some things that children do that upset others (e.g., tattle all the time, break promises, boss you around, tease you, use put downs, lie, have to be the center of attention, are selfish, hit and kick). If using puppets, have students hold up their puppets when the characters' names are mentioned so other students can see which animal is talking. Tell students to listen to the story about the Sunshine Elementary students and watch for which character shows friendly behavior and which character does not.

Friendship

Lilly Lambkin was really sad and even Lucky couldn't cheer her up. Tabby was gone and Lilly didn't know where she was!

"I let her out last night and this morning she didn't come for her food," Lilly told her mother, almost in tears.

"Honey, Tabby is a smart cat and she probably just went visiting and will be back when you get home from school," Mrs. Lambkin said. "Now, hurry up and get ready to go to school."

At school, Lilly was really quiet and at recess she just sat on the swing and didn't talk to anyone. Her friend, Cherry Chicken, came up and said, "What a sourpuss you are, Lilly. What on earth is wrong with you today?"

"Tabby, my cat, is gone and I'm afraid something happened to her," said Lilly.

"Really," said Cherry as she ran off to play as if she didn't even care about Lilly.

"Golly, I'm sorry," said Susie Squirrel as she came over and sat on the swing beside Lilly. Soon they both were swinging and talking.

"I'm afraid something has happened to her," said Lilly. "I'm really worried about her."

Then Lilly stopped swinging suddenly, got off the swing and went walking on the grass by the Sunshine Elementary School building. Susie quickly got off, too, and hurried up to walk beside Lilly. She knew her friend was sad and wanted to make her feel better. "Has Tabby ever been gone overnight before?" asked Susie.

"Oh," exclaimed Lilly. "Yes, she has. I remember now. Last summer she stayed out all night and didn't come home until the next afternoon."

"See, she will probably be there today when you get home after school," said Susie. "I'll call you when I get home to see if Tabby is back."

"You're probably right," said Lilly, perking up a little.

"There's nothing you can do right now and worrying doesn't really help so let's go jump rope for a while," suggested Susie.

The two first graders went off to get a jump rope from the teacher.

That night when Lilly got home from school, guess who met her on the steps? You're right, it was Tabby and Lilly hugged her as she went inside. The phone rang right then and Lilly answered it. It was Susie asking if Tabby was home yet and Lilly said, "Yes, and she was so glad to see me." Then Lilly thought for a minute and said, "Susie, you are a good friend. You really cared about how I felt today. Thank you."

⚠? Discussion Questions

1. Why was Lilly sad? (Tabby did not come home.)

2. Was Cherry a good friend? (No) Why? (She used a put down on Lilly and didn't talk to her about being sad or try to cheer her up.)

3. Was Susie a good friend? (Yes) Why? (She listened to Lilly and talked with her about why she was sad and helped her feel better.)

4. What was the difference between Cherry's and Susie's behavior. (Susie was a good friend because she acted like she cared about Lilly and Cherry didn't.)

5. Tell about a time when you helped someone when they needed a friend.

☆ Activities

1. Have students tell characteristics of a good friend. (Teacher lists them on the board.)
2. Have students pick one characteristic and draw and color a picture showing it.

☆ Role Play

How would you show you are a good friend if . . .

1. One of your friends asked you to go to the movies, then canceled it when you were really looking forward to it.
2. You were playing a game with Lisa and you were losing.
3. You promised to go to the mall with Joni but Lisa asked you to go to the movies with her instead and you really wanted to see the movie.
4. Tom accidentally bumped you when you were playing ball and it really hurt when you fell down.
5. Richard grabbed your paper and you thought about telling the teacher.
6. Jimmy is having trouble learning his math.
7. The teacher asked you to show the new student around.
8. Max and Justin were picking on Rusty.
9. Beth was saying put-downs to Jamie.
10. Jill wants to tell you secrets about Sue.

☑ Lesson 17: Playing Fair

Playing Fair — To play fair means to follow the rules
and not to cheat or change the rules and to always
act honorably whether you win or lose.

It is our responsibility to play fair. If we want others to trust us and continue to play with us, then we will always follow the rules, take our turn when it is really our turn, and not change the rules in the middle of the game so we can win. Winning is fun, but it is not worth cheating or losing friends for. Playing fair means that we try our best to win, but we know that it is not always possible to win so we try not to get upset when we lose because we know there will always be another game to play. It is important to play fair because we should think about our friends and how we would feel if they didn't play fair. Others lose respect for us if we continually whine about losing or we continually try to get extra turns or crowd into a line. Playing fair is an important part of our responsibility to ourselves and to others.

Directions: Read and discuss introduction. Then briefly discuss some examples of responsible behavior. (Do chores, work at school, obey parents, take responsibility when you have an accident, and be honest.) Ask what responsibility has to do with playing fair. (It is our responsibility to know how to play fair.) If using puppets have students hold up the puppets when their characters' names are mentioned so the other students can see which character is talking. Tell students to listen carefully to the story so they will be able to tell what the students from Sunshine Elementary School learned about playing fair.

Playing Tag

It was a really nice day after several days of dismal rain and everyone was really happy to be outside and run around on the playground. At noon recess after eating, the excitement was great and all the students wanted to play games. The friends didn't even stop to talk before Cherry Chicken yelled, "Let's play tag. Doolee Dog, you're IT," and she touched him and quickly ran away.

Before you could snap your fingers, everyone scattered all over the playground, trying not to be tagged. Cherry, being small, was really good at getting away from people and she laughed as Doolee sneaked up on Lilly Lambkin and touched her, "You're IT," he yelled and away he ran.

Lilly wasn't particularly good at tag but she ran this way and that, trying to tag someone. She missed her brother, Lucky Lambkin, by a good four feet and Ted Turkey just gobbled at her as he danced away from her. Finally, Lilly got Minnie Moo and said, "You're IT" getting away just in time to sit for a minute and rest.

Minnie turned quickly and touched Ronnie Rabbit, who was always hard to catch because he was fast but he had been watching Lilly and laughing. Good-naturedly, Ronnie went hopping after Susie but she ran up a tree and Ronnie yelled, "No fair. You can't go up trees in tag" so Susie giggled and showed she was a good sport and came on down. Ronnie tagged her then and off he went. Susie was IT. She went scurrying after Lucky who was watching Cherry hiding behind the bushes so Susie touched Lucky and he was IT.

With a laugh, Lucky went after Corky Colt figuring he would really have to sneak up on him because Corky was probably the fastest runner in first grade. Corky acted real smart and would stop and tease Lucky and then when Lucky just about touched him, Corky would take off. One time, though, Corky's foot slipped in a mud puddle and Lucky got him. Corky just laughed; he thought the game was fun and he liked taking a turn at being IT. He had been watching Cherry hiding behind others and so off he went after Cherry.

Cherry saw him coming and she decided she didn't want to be IT, at least not right now, so she went over to the playground teacher and asked what time it was.

Corky saw Cherry do this and decided to touch her anyway so he did. "You're IT," he said.

"I can't be," said Cherry. "I was talking to the teacher."

Corky laughed, shook his head and went after Ted Turkey, catching him really fast.

Ted, who was enjoying the game, just giggled and headed off after Kathy Kat. Kathy tried to get away from Ted, by dodging around Billy Goat, but Ted got her anyway, "You're IT." Kathy decided she would just have to go after someone else.

Kathy ran and ran around the playground and was really getting tired when she caught Billy Goat who was busy talking to Corky and hadn't noticed her sneaking up behind him.

Billy looked around. There was Cherry Chicken, laughing as she talked to Lilly and he thought, she started this, it's time to get her to be IT. He went after both little friends, laughing as they both split up and started running. Just then he slipped in a puddle and reached out and barely reached Cherry, saying, "You're IT."

"Oh, no, I'm not," Cherry said. "You missed me." And off she went. Billy was pretty sure he had touched her so he asked Lilly, "Didn't I touch her?"

"It sure looked like it," said Lilly.

Billy pulled a surprise move and reached out and really got Cherry. "Now, you can't say you weren't touched. You're IT." and off he went.

Cherry stomped her foot, "That wasn't fair. I was just watching and not playing. You needed to warn me." She runs over and stomps in a puddle right beside Billy and splashes him with muddy water.

Lilly looked at Cherry as all the friends came over, "Cherry, that's not nice. You didn't play fair. Maybe we shouldn't let you play tag anymore."

Corky, still feeling excited about the game, said, "Cherry, Lilly, it's just a game. We shouldn't fight over a silly game. Cherry, being tagged IT is fun. You can't change the rules or hide behind a teacher or pretend you didn't get tagged. Everyone has to take their turn being IT when they get tagged or it isn't fair. And Lilly, how is Cherry going to learn to be a good sport and play fair if we don't let her play and learn?"

Lilly looked at Cherry and said, "Will you play tag the fair way if we let you play some more?"

Cherry put her head down and said, "Corky, you are right. I really don't mind being IT, I just don't like to admit when I get tagged. I know I sometimes do this in games and I will try not to do it any more. I like my friends who will forgive me and let me play."

She stood in the middle and said, "Okay, I'm IT. You guys had better get going."

⚠ Discussion Questions

1. Were all the students playing fair? (No, Cherry was trying to get out of being IT.)

2. What was Cherry doing? (She stood by the teacher, tried to change the rules, and later said she wasn't touched when she was.)

3. How do you think the others felt when they were playing fair and Cherry wasn't? (They didn't like it. Lilly didn't want Cherry to play any more.)

4. Was Cherry thinking about her friends when she wasn't playing fair? (No, she was thinking about herself.)

5. What made Cherry decide she should start playing fair? (Corky talked about how much fun the game was and he said Cherry should learn to be a good sport and play fair.)

6. Did Cherry ever admit that she wasn't playing fair? (Yes, she said she didn't like to admit when she got tagged and she would try to be better if they let her keep playing.)

7. Tell about when you were playing a game and someone didn't play fair? How did you feel?

8. Tell about a time when you didn't play fair? How did you feel? How do you think the others felt? What would you do differently next time?

Activities

1. Draw a picture of students playing a game and color the one who is not playing fair.

2. Draw a picture of students playing a game and color the ones who are playing fair.

Role Play

How would you handle the following situations . . .

1. You and your friend are playing marbles and he won three of yours but you refuse to give them to him.

2. Everyone is in line to play ball and Freddy pushes in front of you.

3. Lisa and you decide to swing but there is only one swing open so she says she will swing for a while then you can, but she won't give up the swing.

4. You are playing checkers with a friend and he leaves the game to get a drink. You really want to change some of the checkers around.

5. You are playing jump rope and you missed so it's someone else's turn, but you want to keep jumping.

6. At home, it's your turn to do dishes, but you're trying to tell your mom that it's your brother's turn.

7. You and your friends are playing tag on the playground and the rule is that anyone can play. Mark wants to play and you tell him "no."

8. You are playing kickball and you are touched before you get to first base but you refuse to go out.

9. You are playing the card game Crazy Eights with a friend and you want to sneak a card out of the deck.

10. You are playing a computer game and it's your sister's turn, but you refuse to let her play.

✓ Lesson 18: Feeling Left Out

Feeling Left Out – Feeling left out is when you are
not invited to play or join in games or other
activities and it makes you feel sad.

It is our responsibility to have what we call empathy for others and invite them to play when they are feeling left out. Empathy means to understand how others feel or understand how you would feel if you were in their place. Students who come to a new school often feel left out until someone invites them to join their group of friends. Others might feel left out if they are not included in a game, party, or group activity. Being able to see when people feel left out is important. Someone standing alone and looking sad might mean the person is feeling left out. It is our responsibility to go talk to them or include them in what we are doing. We need be able to understand how they are feeling because we know how we would feel if we were in their place. No one likes to be left out but all of us have felt that way once in a while. We can also take the responsibility of going up to a group or a friend and asking to join them if we feel left out.

Directions: Read and discuss the introduction. Ask students what they have been learning about responsibility and give some examples of responsible behavior. (Do chores at home, work at school, obey parents, be honest, help others, and admit if we break a rule rather than blaming others.) Ask what responsibility has to do with helping people feel a part of a group. (It is our responsibility to notice how others feel and think about how we would feel if we were in their place.) Discuss how to recognize when people are feeling left out. Tell students to look around them and if they see a student who is standing apart from others and no one is talking to them, then they are probably feeling alone and left out. Sometimes this means we will have to leave our group and go over to the person. It can be rewarding because we may find a new friend who is fun to play with and needs a chance to get to know us. Listen carefully to the story and see how the students at Sunshine Elementary learn to prevent people from feeling left out. (If using puppets, have students hold the puppets up as their characters' names are read.)

The Visitor at Sunshine Elementary

Miss Lion seemed really excited one day as she told about a little friend who would be visiting Sunshine Elementary for the next few weeks. She introduced Tiny Tiger who was in the United States with his parents for a two-week visit. She said Tiny was also a first grader and wanted to visit her class. She had Tiny talk about his school, Angola Grade School in Africa and he said there were only six students in his class. He said he was learning to read and to print and he thought school was fun.

70

Miss Lion had Tiny sit in front of Lucky Lambkin and then started the class. All the children got busy coloring a picture and then they practiced printing their names.

"Hey, Tiny. what are you printing?" Lucky said as he looked over Tiny's shoulder. Tiny said, "My name."

"It looks funny," said Lucky. "You talk kind of funny, too."

"That's because I am from Africa," Tiny said with his African accent.

"But Miss Lion doesn't talk funny," said Lucky.

They had to quit talking just then as Miss Lion looked at them with her "be quiet" look.

At recess, Tiny tried to walk out with Lucky but didn't get into line soon enough. All the kids ran to play kickball and Tiny didn't know what they were doing so he just stood there and watched. No one noticed but Miss Lion and she went over to Tiny and talked to him in his own language. She asked him why he wasn't playing and he told her he didn't know what the students were doing. She said, in English, "Don't worry. I'm sure someone will come and help you learn the game." Suddenly, Susie Squirrel fell down and cried that she was hurt, so Miss Lion had to rush over to help Susie and take her inside to get first aid for a nasty looking cut.

Tiny just stood there for most of the recess.

Then Ted Turkey stopped playing ball for a minute and said to Lucky, "Hey, your friend Tiny is just standing there. Do you think we should go ask him to play?"

"Golly, it's hard to understand him," said Lucky, "but I guess we should do that."

So the two boys went over to Tiny and asked him if he wanted to play kickball.

"I don't know how," said Tiny but he kind of muttered it and with his accent the boys didn't understand him.

Lucky looked at Ted and said, "What did he say?"

"Geez, I don't know, but I don't think he wants to play," said Ted.

The boys turned to leave but just then Cherry came up. "Hey, did you get Tiny to come play?"

"Naw, he doesn't seem to want to," said Ted.

"Don't be silly," said Cherry with a flip of her head. "He probably doesn't know what you want him to do. I'll bet he feels left out because he didn't understand you and you know how any of us would feel if no one asked us to play. Let me talk to him."

She went up to Tiny and said, "Come on, Tiny. You can learn how to play the game. We'll show you," and she grabbed his hand and off they went back to the game.

"Hey, you guys, let's stop and go through how we play the game," Cherry said and Lucky and Ted looked at each other as they started to explain, "Okay, Tiny. First the person up gets to kick the ball and then run to that base out there before someone gets the ball. If the runner gets there before the ball, they stay there until someone else kicks the ball and then they run to second base." Lucky and Ted proceed to show Tiny how to play the game and before long, Tiny had caught on.

Everybody said since Tiny was a visitor, he got to be up first. Tiny gave the ball a mighty kick and ran to first. Everybody cheered for him. As he stood on first he looked around and grinned.

Just then Miss Lion and Susie came back outside and Miss Lion looked pleased that Tiny was playing. She thought, I'm glad the class has enough feelings of empathy and understanding to help others who are feeling left out.

⚠ Discussion Questions

1. What is empathy? (It is understanding the feelings of others.)

2. Why was Tiny feeling left out? (He didn't know how to play the game.)

3. What did Lucky and Ted do? (They went to Tiny and asked him to play.)

4. Why didn't Tiny play when Lucky and Ted asked him? (He said he didn't know how to play but they couldn't understand him.)

5. What did Cherry do? (She told Ted and Lucky that Tiny probably didn't understand them either and she just took Tiny's hand and led him back to the rest of the students. This showed Tiny that they wanted him.)

6. What did Ted and Lucky do then? (They actually demonstrated the game for Tiny.)

7. Tell of a time when you have been left out of a game or activity and how you felt.

8. Tell of a time when you invited someone to play because you knew they were feeling sad because they were feeling left out. (You had empathy for them.)

✄ Activities

1. Draw a picture of Tiny Tiger feeling happy because he just learned how to play kickball.

2. Draw a picture of how you can tell when someone is feeling left out.

🧎 Role Play

How would you show empathy in the following situations . . .

1. Mary is having a bad day and just sitting on the swing watching the rest of the students play.

2. Jennifer is standing behind Charlie and Lisa as they play on the computer and pretty soon she goes over and sits down.

3. Bonnie is crying because she fell down and no one noticed.

4. Will was last out for recess because he was looking at the bad grade he got on his paper.

5. When the children chose sides for a game, Jill is always last to be picked so she just stood along side the corner of the school building looking sad.

6. Fred sprained his ankle last week and couldn't play kickball this week.

7. Tommy asked all his friends to come to his birthday party, but didn't invite Andy.

8. Mom took your sister shopping and you have to stay home and finish the dishes.

9. Two big boys from third grade are picking on Fred and you see it.

10. Jimmy wants you to go to the movies with him but you have already asked Al to come play at your home.

☑ Lesson 19: Refusal Skills

> Refusal Skills — Refusal skills are skills that help you say "no." They also help you have some control over your life and actions and saying "no" sometimes helps prevent you from getting into trouble.

Saying "no" is sometimes hard, especially when your friends are encouraging you to do something that sounds like fun or they make it sound so good that you really think you want to do it. Refusal skills involve the ability to know when a situation is wrong or has possible negative consequences.

- This means you need to learn to say "no."
- To keep friends, you should know how to come up with another activity or change the subject.
- If you must, you should know how to just walk away.
- Learning to use refusal skills is your responsibility.

Directions: Read and discuss introduction. Ask students what they have learned this year about practicing responsible behavior. Ask students what knowing how to say no, using refusal skills, has to do with responsibility. (It is the student's responsibility to know some ways to avoid getting involved in activities that will get them into trouble.) If using puppets, select students to represent the characters in the story and have them stand so they can be seen by the other students. After giving out the puppets, explain that when they hear their character (puppet) talk in the story, they are to raise the puppet so the other students can see which animal is talking. Tell the students to listen to the story so they will be able to tell how the animal friends used refusal skills to stay out of trouble.

Refusal Skills

Kathy Kat and Cherry Chicken were playing at Kathy's home when Mrs. Kat asked Kathy if she and Cherry wanted to go to the store to get a half-gallon of milk to go with the cookies she was baking.

At the store the two little girls picked out the milk. As they went toward the checkout aisle, they saw Doolee Dog and Ted Turkey standing nearby.

"We're running an errand for my mother," said Kathy. "What are you guys doing?"

"We're picking out candy bars. Hey, Ted, I found two I like but I only have money for one. Which one shall I pick, a Peanut Butter Reese cup or a chocolate Hershey bar?" Doolee said.

Ted laughed and said, "Take them both. No one will see if you put one under your coat."

Doolee looked funny. "But that's stealing and I shouldn't do that."

Ted said, "Not if they don't catch you."

Kathy and Cherry looked at each other. "That's stealing and it's against the law whether anyone catches you or not," said Kathy and Cherry nodded her head and said, "You could go to jail and we would get into trouble because we are with you."

Ted said, "Don't be silly. No one would send a little kid to jail for taking a Peanut Butter Reese Cup and Doolee really wants it. It's his most favorite."

"I don't know," said Doolee. "The girls are probably right. It is stealing if you take something without paying for it."

"I have an idea," said Kathy. "Why don't we go to my house and have some cookies and milk. Mom was making cookies when we left and they are peanut butter cookies so they will be really good."

"Right," said Cherry.

"Yum. That sounds good," said Doolee, "and you are right, we shouldn't take things without paying for them."

"Let's go," agreed Ted. "I guess you are right. That is stealing. I'm sorry and I would like to go to your house, Kathy."

"We can play a computer game after we have the cookies and milk," said Kathy as the four of them went through the check-out counter to pay for the milk and neither Ted nor Doolee even got a candy bar.

⚠ Discussion Questions

1. What did Ted try to talk Doolee into doing? (Stealing a candy bar)

2. What did Kathy say to Ted and Doolee about taking the candy bar without paying for it? (That's stealing and it's against the law.)

3. What did Cherry say about it? (They would all get into trouble because they are together.)

4. How did Kathy get the boys interested in doing something else so they weren't even thinking about stealing? (She suggested going to her house for cookies and milk and playing a computer game later.)

5. If Doolee hadn't listened to Kathy and decided to steal the candy bar, what should Kathy and Cherry have done? (Walk away)

6. Tell about a time that someone wanted you to do something that you knew wasn't right or was against the law. How did you handle it? What did you tell them to change their mind or did you do it?

✗ Activities

1. Draw a picture of a time when somebody wanted you to do something that was against the law or that you knew your parents wouldn't like.

2. Draw a picture of one of the three refusal skills (say no, come up with a different activity to do, or walk away). Option: may post on wall.

✗ Role Play

How would you practice refusal skills if . . .

1. Joey saw a bicycle in a yard as he was walking home with Freddy and decided he wanted to take it for a ride.

2. Susie was having fun with Patty throwing dirt clods in the rain puddle when the new kid, Freddy, came along the sidewalk and Susie said, "Let's throw dirt clods at him."

3. Joey and Freddy were playing at Freddy's home when they found a gun in a drawer and Freddy suggested that they play cops and robbers.

4. Susie and Patty were helping to clean their mother's bedroom when they found an open pack of cigarettes and a lighter and Patty suggested they smoke one.

5. Joey and Freddy were hungry and Freddy looked into the cabinet and found a half-filled bottle of whiskey. Joey suggested they "have a drink."

6. Freddy and Joey were playing in the living room as their dad was watching television. When he fell asleep, Joey thought it would be fun to "sneak" a few sips of their dad's beer.

7. Susie and Patty were walking home from the store when a car pulled up and a man leaned out the window and offered them a ride.

8. Richard, Lou's big brother, asked Lou and Tom if they wanted some pills.

9. Tom didn't know how to spell the words on the spelling test so he wanted to copy Lou's paper.

10. Tom forgot his lunch money and wanted Lou's.

✓ Lesson 20: Handling Bullies

> Bullies — A bully is someone who teases, frightens, threatens, or hurts smaller or weaker people. Handling means using ways to deal with a bully.

Handling bullies takes the ability to think clearly without reacting in an emotional way. If you cry or yell, this encourages the bully because that's what they want you to do. You must always take the responsibility for your actions but you must remember that you are not responsible for a bully's behavior. Their actions are always his or her problem, not yours. There are four steps you can take to help you handle the way bullies behave:

1. Ignore them and walk away (do not call names back).

2. Assert yourself: stand tall and look them in the eye and say, "Stop it! I don't like it when you treat me that way."

3. Ask for help from some adult if the bully continues hurting or threatening you.

4. Self-talk: tell yourself "that's the bully's problem and I'm okay. I am a special person. I am good at making friends." (At this point the teacher might want to have each of the students name something that they can use when they want to do positive self-talk.)

Directions: Read and discuss introduction and list the four steps to handling a bully on the board or poster. Briefly review some examples of responsible behavior. (Do chores, work at school, obey parents, take responsibility when you have an accident, and be honest.) Ask what responsibility has to do with handling a bully. (It is our responsibility to know how to handle a bully so we can take care of ourselves and our feelings.) If using puppets for the following story, select students to represent characters in the story as the teacher reads it. Tell students to listen to the story so they can tell if the animal friends know how to use the four steps to handling bullies.

Handling Bullies

One day after school, Lucky and Lilly Lambkin and all their friends met out on the playground to walk to Kathy Kat's house for her birthday party. They were all excited and chattering about the games they would play when they suddenly realized that Kathy Kat was missing.

"I'll go look for her," said Lilly as she headed back to the school-house door. The others watched and saw her stop to talk to Kathy who was sitting on the steps. Lilly looked up and yelled, "Come here, guys, there's something wrong."

First Grade Lesson 20: HANDLING BULLIES

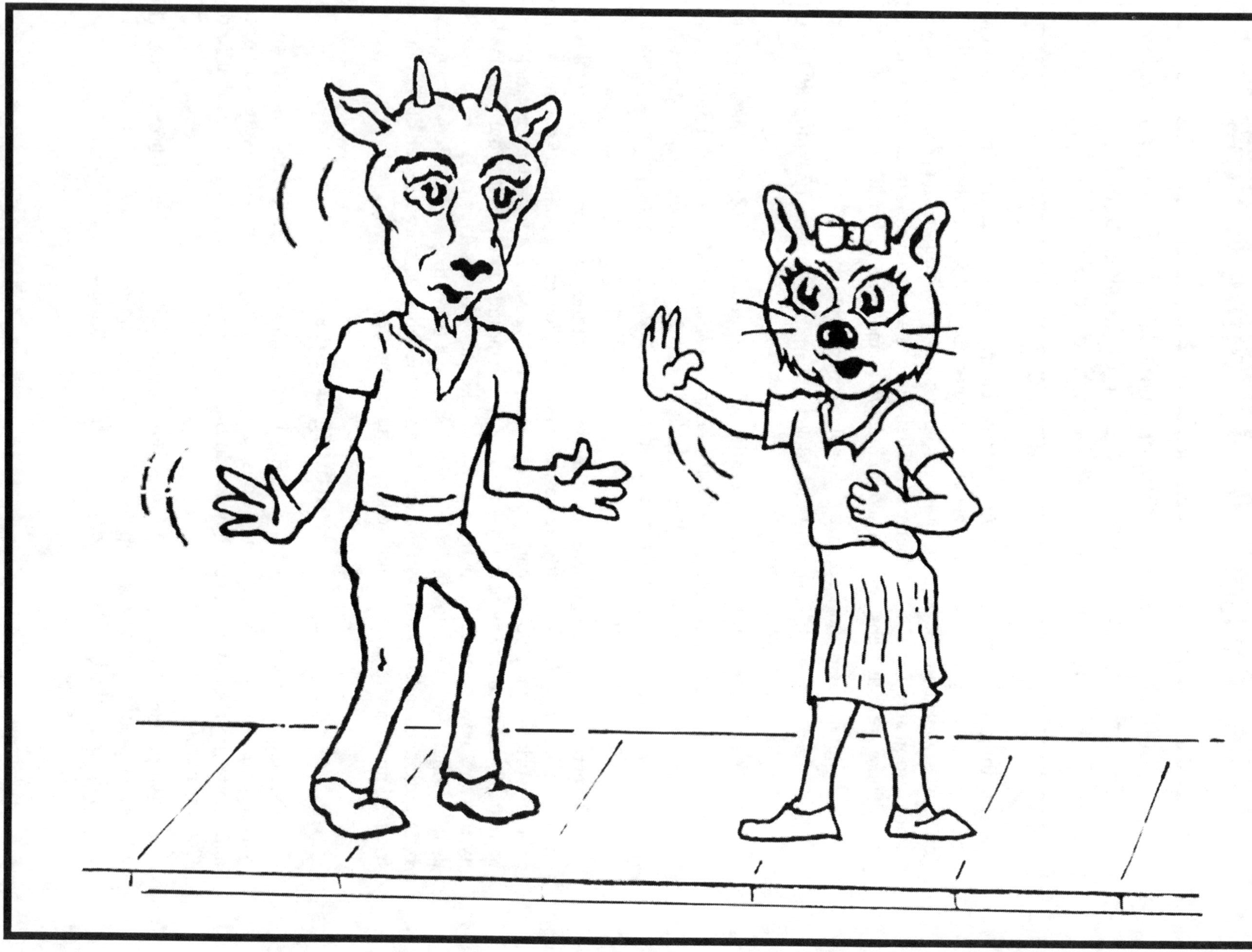

As they all ran toward Lilly and Kathy they could see Kathy was crying.

"What's wrong?" said Lucky, Susie, and Ronnie, all together.

Kathy was sobbing and couldn't answer so Lilly answered for her. "That big bully, Billy Goat, tripped her and called her names like he always does."

Ted Turkey, Corky Colt, and Doolee Dog were all ready to go find Billy and beat him up, but Lilly said, "You can't do that. Then you would be bullies too. That's silly."

"The first thing we should do is ignore him and walk away," said Cherry Chicken as she looked around. "So what was the next step Mrs. Owl told us to do to handle a bully?"

Lilly said, "Kathy, if Billy ever tries that again, you have to stand tall and say, 'I don't like it when you call me names and trip me.' Then you need to walk away. Can you do that? And if he keeps threatening you or tries to hurt you, you need to get help from an adult right away."

"I'll try," said Kathy sniffling. "Then I can do the self-talk, because it is his problem not mine. I know I am a good friend to others and I have lots of friends like all of you guys. I guess I'm okay now. Let's go to my house and have the party."

The friends had a good time at the party and went home with full tummies and laughing about all the fun games they played.

The next morning as Lilly and Lucky were almost to the school door, they saw Billy Goat go up to Kathy Kat and say something to her. They ran as fast as they could to get near enough to Kathy to help her, but they could see that she was handling the bully.

Billy said, "You creepy little kitty, why do you think you are so smart? I'm going to trip you again and watch you cry."

Kathy stood tall and said, "Stop it! I don't like it when you call me names. That hurts my feelings." Then she turned and, standing tall, walked away, saying to herself, "I know being a bully is his problem, not mine. I didn't do anything wrong. I am a kind girl and have a lot of friends who love me. "

Billy stood there, surprised. His favorite little kitty to pick on had actually stood up to him. Maybe she wasn't such a pushover anymore.

⚠ Discussion Questions

1. Why was Kathy Kat crying? (Billy Goat called her names and tripped her.)

2. What did the friends teach Kathy Kat about handling a bully? (The steps to handling bullies are: a) ignore the bully and walk away, b) assert yourself, stand tall, and say "Stop it! I don't like the way you're treating me," c) tell yourself it's the bully's problem, then tell yourself something that you are good at doing, d) if the bully continues to threaten you or tries to hurt you, get help from an adult.)

3. Whose problem was it that Billy was being mean to Kathy? (It's always the bully's problem.)

4. Why do you think Billy was acting like a bully? (Some reasons people act like bullies are: they have been bullied, they are having a bad day, and/or they are showing off for their friends.)

5. Should Kathy Kat have called Billy Goat names back? (No, never call names or show feelings. This encourages the bully.)

6. What happened the next day when she tried handling the bully? (The steps worked.)

7. Tell about a time when you were bullied by someone, how you handled it, and how you felt.

8. Tell abut a time when someone thought you were a bully.

Activities

1. Draw how it feels to be bullied.
2. Draw how it feels to be a bully.
3. Draw and color a poster showing the four steps to help you handle a bully.

Role Play

How would you practice the four steps for handling a bully if . . .

1. Susie keeps taking your dessert out of your lunch box.
2. Dakota stops you on the way to school and demands your lunch money.
3. Johnny trips you every time you have to walk by his desk.
4. When you sit in front of Billy he ties your hair in knots.
5. Angie calls you names every time she's having a bad day.
6. Lachelle wears your sweater (or coat) when she forgets hers.
7. Austin steals your pencil whenever he breaks his.
8. Tom teases you about having a girl (or boy) friend.
9. Linda takes the swing away from you and pushes you down in the mud.
10. Rob tells you that you have to give him your new ball or he will beat you up.

Optional: Have the students role play some of the things that have happened to them.

☑ Lesson 21: Having a Bad Day

Having a Bad Day — Having a bad day is when everything seems to go wrong, no matter how hard we try.

Some people call them "bad-hair days" but everyone has a bad day now and then. This is a day when something happens, like we break our favorite toy, or can't find anything to wear to school, or our goldfish dies, or our best friend is sick so we miss walking to school together. When we're having a bad day, everything that happens seems to tear away at the special feeling we have for ourselves. Before long the feeling of being lovable and capable that we wake up with, starts going away and we start feeling sad. This doesn't have to happen. We can stop it. The keys to bringing back our feelings of being lovable and capable are:

- Find someone to talk to.
- Self-talk by telling ourselves that we are lovable and capable and good at something like spelling, reading, math, fishing, cooking, or hitting a ball.
- Do something active, like ride our bikes, play ball with a friend, or work on a hobby.

Directions: (It will be necessary to prepare nine post-its with **lovable** and **capable** written on them and assign parts in advance. Parts may need to be performed by other adults or older students.) Ask students what they have been learning about practicing responsible behavior. Ask the students what having a bad day has to do with responsibility. (It is our responsibility to know how to make ourselves feel better when we are having a bad day.) We are in charge of our feelings and also how we react to what happens to us. Explain that everyone is lovable and capable but sometimes things happen that make us feel hurt. Then, something else happens that upsets us and this can go on unless we know to use the three keys to bring back our feelings of being lovable and capable. The teacher then goes over the three keys (see above) and tells the students we are going to perform a skit with first graders. The teacher explains that she will play Betsy, who is a first grader, as she gets out the nine post-its on which are written **lovable** and **capable.** (She sticks the post-its all over her shirt. As each negative thing happens to Betsy, teacher will drop one post-it to the floor. She then hands out the parts and sets the scene by reading the following.) Betsy always wakes up in the morning feeling lovable and capable. Watch the skit to see if Betsy has a good day and keeps her good feelings or if she has a bad day and learns how to handle it.

Lovable-and-Capable Skit

Teacher sets the scene by saying: We will follow Betsy through her day and see what happens. The skit opens in Betsy's room at her home as she is getting ready to go to school where she is in the first grade.

Betsy:	I can't believe I can't find my favorite T-shirt. What am I going to wear to school today. Sarah and I both agreed to wear our blue T-shirts. Mom, have you seen my blue T-shirt?
Mother:	Yes, you put it in the wash and I'm washing it now.
Betsy:	Mother, how could you do that? I need it to wear today.
Mother:	Well, you should have told me. Wear something else. Hurry or you will be late.

(Betsy drops a post-it to the floor.)

Betsy:	Hi, little goldfish. here is your food. Oh, no, Little Goldie is floating on the top of the water. She's dead! Oh, Bonnie, my goldfish died.
Bonnie:	Hey, little sister, you should have fed it yesterday.

(Betsy drops another post-it on the floor.)

Betsy:	What kind of cereal are you eating?
Bonnie:	I'm eating Lucky Crunchies but there isn't any more because you ate most of them yesterday.

(Betsy drops another post-it to the floor.)

Betsy:	Go-l- l-e-e. What am I going to eat now?
Bonnie:	That's your problem but I hear the bus honking and here comes dad.
Father:	Betsy, don't miss the bus. You know it's your responsibility to catch the bus and I had to take you to school two days last week.

(Betsy drops another post-it to the floor.)

Betsy:	Well, I made it on the bus. There's Sarah. Hi, Sarah, can I sit with you?
Sarah:	No, I'm saving a seat. Where's your blue T-shirt you promised to wear? I have mine on. You sure didn't keep your word.

(Betsy drops another post-it to the floor.)

Betsy:	Well, I'm finally at school. Hi, teacher.
Teacher:	Hello, Betsy, did you remember your reading book?
Betsy:	Golly, I was late and I forgot.

Teacher:	This is the third day in a row you were supposed to bring it. It's your responsibility to remember it.

(Betsy drops another post-it to the floor.)

Betsy:	Oh, good, let's go play. It's recess time.
Bobbie:	No, Betsy, you can't play. You throw like a baby.

(Betsy drops another post-it on the floor.)

Betsy:	Nobody likes me. I guess I'll just go sit by myself.

(Betsy drops another post-it on the floor.)

Teacher:	Everybody come on in. Let's work on our cards for our parents.
Betsy:	Oh, mine ripped. I'm so clumsy.

(Betsy drops another post-it on the floor.)

Betsy:	Mom, Bonnie, I'm home.
Bonnie:	Have some cookies and milk.
Betsy:	Gee, that tastes good. What a day!
Bonnie:	Bad day, huh?
Betsy:	Yes. My blue T-shirt was in the wash. My goldfish died. There was no more Lucky Crunchies. I was almost late. Sarah wouldn't sit with me on the bus. I forgot my reading book. Bobbie wouldn't let me play and I accidentally tore my card for mom and dad. It was really a bad day.
Bonnie:	Boy, that does sound like a bummer of a day. We all have bad days once in a while. My school counselor taught us a really cool way to feel lovable and capable after having a bad day. It's three simple things: Talk about it. Tell yourself you're good at something. Go do something active.

*(As Bonnie talks, Betsy picks up a couple of post-it notes
and sticks them back on her blouse.)*

Betsy:	Wow! That sounds great. I think I'll try it. I'm already talking to you. I really am good at riding my bike and I think I'll go out and ride it right now.

⚠ Discussion Questions

1. Did Betsy keep her lovable and capable feelings all day? (No)

2. What are some of the things that happened? (Blue T-shirt was in the wash. Goldfish died. There was no more Lucky Crunchies. Betsy was running late. Sarah wouldn't sit with her on the bus. She forgot her reading book. Bobbie wouldn't let her play. She accidentally tore her card.)

3. Did she start to feel lovable and capable again? If so, when? (Talking to Bonnie, self-talk, and activity.)

4. What are the three keys to keeping lovable and capable feelings? (Find someone to talk to. Self-talk by telling ourselves that we are lovable and capable and good at something like spelling, reading, math, fishing, cooking, or hitting a ball. Do something active, like ride our bikes, play ball with a friend, or work on a hobby.

5. Tell about a time you had a bad day. Tell which of the three keys you used to feel lovable and capable again.

6. What is the most important one of the three keys to learn how to do? (Find someone to talk with.) Who can you talk to?

7. Name one thing you can say you're good at when you're having a bad day? (Make list and save for role play.)

8. Name some activities that you can do to bring back the lovable and capable feeling? (Make a list and save for role play.)

✗ Activities

1. Draw a picture of you using at least one of the three keys.
2. Draw a poster of the three keys.

✗ Role Play

Show how you would keep your lovable and capable feelings if . . .

1. Johnny called you a name.
2. Your goldfish died.
3. Your best friend wouldn't let you sit with her on the bus.
4. Mom said you weren't responsible because you forgot to feed the dog.
5. Teacher got angry at you because you didn't bring your reading book to school.
6. You couldn't find your favorite shirt.
7. Your best friend played with someone else at recess.
8. You didn't get invited to Sally's birthday party.
9. Trying to ride your bike, you keep falling off.
10. You got a bad grade on your arithmetic test.

☑ **Lesson 22: Making Good Choices**

> Making Good Choices — Making good choices is the
> ability to choose appropriate actions or behavior
> when offered different selections.

We are faced with choices all the time in our everyday life. We have to choose how much of our lunch we are going to eat, who to play with, what games to play, what clothes to wear, and what toys we want. Often adults give us choices or a chance to participate in choosing things like what we want to eat, where we want to go on vacation, what activity we want to do, what kind of haircut we want, and many others. Life is full of choices even when we are young. It is our responsibility to learn how to make good choices because it will help keep us safe, have friends, get good grades, and feel proud of ourselves. Making good choices is not always easy because we don't always know what makes some decisions good or bad. Sometimes when we are young we make mistakes in our choices, but that is how we learn. The important thing is to take the responsibility to learn to make good choices so that when we grow up we can do it easily.

The questions to ask yourself about possible choices are:

- Will it hurt anyone?
- Will it be breaking rules?

Directions: Review what students have been learning about responsibility. Ask students what responsibility has to do with making good decisions. (We are responsible for the choices we make and the results of those choices.) Read and discuss introduction and review the questions students should ask themselves when they have a difficult decision to make. (Will this choice hurt anyone? Will this choice be breaking rules?) If using puppets, select students to hold up their puppets as the characters' names are read. Tell the students that in the following lesson, Doolee Dog will have to make a choice. Tell them to listen carefully so they will be able to help him make a good choice.

A Choice

Lucky Lambkin and Doolee Dog were playing at Doolee's house when Mrs. Dog had to go to a meeting and she asked Doolee if he thought he and Lucky were old enough to take care of his little sister, Daisy, for an hour.

Doolee said, "Sure, I'm almost seven and Lucky is here to help me."

Mrs. Dog looked at Lucky and said, "Do you mind?"

Lucky said, "No, I have a sister at home so I know about girls."

Mrs. Dog smiled and said, "All right. I'll write down the telephone number of where I'll be and I will be home in an hour. You boys can have some cupcakes and soda and see that Daisy gets some. Thanks a lot." Then she left.

Daisy said, "I want something to eat."

The two boys got out the cupcakes and soda and gave some to Daisy. As they were eating, the phone rang and Doolee answered it. Billy Goat was on the phone, real excited about his new race track set and said he couldn't wait for Billy and Lucky to come see it. Doolee told him that they couldn't come over because they were babysitting his sister. Billy said, "Oh, please come over. It wouldn't take long since I live near you." Doolee said he would talk it over with Lucky.

Doolee turned to Lucky and said, "Billy has a new race track set and he wants us to come see it. He's really excited about it and it's one of those fancy new ones where the cars make the loop within a loop. He told me yesterday that he was going to get it. Gosh, it would be fun to go see it for just a minute, don't you think?"

Lucky said, "Wow! It sounds great. I saw a picture of one like that in the catalog. I would really like to see it."

"He lives really close, only two blocks away," said Doolee. "It would only take us a little time to run over there, look at it and come back."

Lucky asked, "But, what will we do with Daisy? We can't take her with us. She's too little and walks too slow."

"Well," said Doolee, "We could put her in the backyard with one of her dolls and another cupcake and she could play house. We'd be back before she even knew we were gone."

Lucky said, "Yeah, we could run really fast."

(The teacher interrupts the story and asks the students what they think the two boys will do. Then, have the students discuss the two questions about making choices to help them advise Doolee and Lucky on choices. Will it hurt anyone? Will it be breaking rules? Then the teacher says, "Let's continue the story to see if Lucky and Doolee make a good decision.")

The boys get Daisy all set up in the backyard and head for the gate. Doolee looked back at Daisy, happily feeding her cupcake to her favorite doll, then came to an abrupt halt. "I can't do this," said Doolee. "What if Daisy got hurt while we were gone? What were the two questions the teacher taught us we're suppose to ask ourselves when we're not sure about a choice we're making?"

"Yeah, you're probably right," answered Lucky. "The two questions we ask ourselves when we have to make a hard decision are: Will it hurt anyone? Will it be breaking the rules?"

"Well, we would sure be breaking the rules if we left Daisy alone because she might fall down and break a leg while we're gone," said Doolee. "She is only four and bad things could happen to her."

"Your mom will be home soon and then we can ask to go see Billy's new race track," said Lucky.

"All right," yelled Doolee relieved that they had made a good choice. I'll race you to the swing set."

⚠ Discussion Questions

1. What was Lucky's and Doolee's responsibility? (Babysit Daisy.)
2. What other choice did Billy Goat give them? (Come see his race set.)
3. What two questions did Lucky and Doolee ask when they were making their decision? (Will it hurt anyone? Will it be breaking rules?)
4. Did Lucky and Doolee make the decision we thought they should make?
5. Tell about a time that you had a hard choice to make? Was it a good decision? Why?

🏃 Activity

1. Have students draw a poster illustrating the two questions for making good decisions. (Option: Post on bulletin board.)

🧎 Role Play

How would you practice making good choices if . . .

Guide students in asking the following two questions for each role play:

- Will it hurt anyone?
- Will it be breaking rules?

1. Jon wants you to help him steal a bike.
2. Jill wants to copy your paper.
3. Your mom is not home and your sister wants you to watch television before the dishes are done.
4. You are having a birthday party and you've invited everyone in your class except Debra.
5. Bob wants you to take a short cut home down a strange alley.
6. Lisa wants you to go to the river and go wading.

7. Playing hide and seek, you consider hiding in the trunk of an old car.

8. Bill wants you to throw rocks at the passing cars.

9. You consider putting your little sister in the old refrigerator.

10. Mom has gone to the store and Sara wants to call her friend long distance.

☑ **Lesson 23: We Can Learn From Our Mistakes**

> Learning from Mistakes — To learn is to gain knowledge or information. A mistake is an error or accident that happens. Learning from mistakes is the ability to gain knowledge after an error or accident happens so that you can avoid that error or accident in the future.

Everyone makes mistakes from time to time. Sometimes we seem to make a lot of mistakes, but that is normal when we are young because we are learning about life. Sometimes we make mistakes because we don't know any better and sometimes we know better but things just seem to happen. Each time we make a mistake, we need to learn from that mistake so that we can either not make it again or know how to handle it if it ever happens again. For example, it may be our responsibility to feed the family dog and because we get busy playing we may make the mistake of forgetting to feed it and everyone seems to get angry with us. We can lie and say we fed the pet or it wasn't our job, but that would not be honest. What we must to do is admit our mistake and correct it. Then remember not to make the same mistake again. We might break something accidentally. When questioned, we might want to lie about it and say we didn't do it, but it is our responsibility to admit it and do what we can to correct it. The mistake would not only be breaking the item, but lying about it and that equals two mistakes.

Directions: Read and discuss the introduction. Ask students what they have learned about responsibility this year. Ask students what responsibility has to do with learning from our mistakes. (It is our responsibility to learn from our mistakes so we can avoid making them again.) Emphasize that everyone makes mistakes but it is how we handle those mistakes that helps others trust us and helps us feel good about ourselves. If using puppets, select students to hold up their puppets as the characters' names are read. Tell the students to listen closely to the following lesson and see if one of the characters makes a mistake and what they would tell him to do about it.

A Mistake

It was Saturday and Corky Colt was a high-spirited young colt. He really wanted to be outside running about in the yard but his mother had told him that he had to help her clean house. She was busy upstairs changing the bed and he was downstairs vacuuming the living room.

Now Corky was perfectly capable of running the vacuum and in the wintertime, he liked doing it. He would pretend he was a space ship and zoom all around the room, being careful to get as far as possible in the galaxy under the couch and in the corners of the room which he called the outer-most depths of space. He really did a good job and his mother always thanked him a lot for helping. In fact, she usually gave him a treat afterwards.

But, today was a beautiful spring day and as Corky vacuumed he looked out the open window and really wanted to be outside, running around playing. He would like to see his friends, Lucky Lambkin and Ronnie Rabbit. He didn't want to be inside at all.

"I can't be a space ship today," Corky muttered to himself as he pushed the big old stupid vacuum around. "It is just a noisy machine and no fun at all," he said. He wasn't being very careful with it either. He rammed it against the couch and pulled it back with a jerk. It ran over his foot which made him even angrier. He pushed again, really hard, and the vacuum hit the legs of the lamp table and over the lamp went. He grabbed for it but missed. The lamp broke.

Corky almost said a bad word. That was his mother's favorite lamp and he knew he was in trouble. He felt bad. What could he do? He didn't know what to do.

(The teacher stops reading and asks the students what they think Corky should do. Help the students come up with possibilities. Possibilities include trying to fix the lamp, telling his mother that the wind came in the open window and knocked the lamp over, just finish the vacuuming leaving the lamp, there and go outside, or go to his mother and tell her he broke the lamp or whatever else the students think of. Help the students decide on what advice they would give Corky, then finish the story.)

Corky knew he had to make up his mind what he should do because his mother would be coming downstairs soon. He thought right away that he would tell her the wind came in the open window and broke the lamp and he tried to catch it but then, he thought, that's not true. I'd be telling a lie.

Corky sat and thought for a minute and remembered what his teacher had said Friday. Miss Lion had told the class that everybody makes mistakes and even has accidents but it was their responsibility to admit their mistakes and that way they could learn from them. She had told them that it was not easy and often people wanted to lie about what happened but that would be another mistake. He remembered her saying, "We must admit what we do and take responsibility for our actions, even when we don't want to."

Just then Mrs. Colt came down the stairway with an armful of sheets. Corky turned off the vacuum and went up to his mother. "Mom," he said, "I was goofing off and accidentally pushed the vacuum into the lamp table and the lamp fell off. I'm sorry. What can I do to fix it?"

"Oh!" said Mrs. Colt as she ran over to the lamp and started picking up the pieces. Then she looked at Corky and even though she really liked the lamp, she saw how upset he was and she said, "Let's see how badly it is broken. Maybe we can mend it."

As they were looking the lamp over at the kitchen table, Corky said, "Gee, Mom, I know how much you liked that lamp. I feel so bad."

"You were careless. I know, because you vacuumed the living room all winter and never broke anything, but you were honest about it and didn't try to lie. That makes me proud," Mrs. Colt said. "Besides, at least it didn't shatter but broke in three big pieces. I think we can glue them back together and it will be fine."

Corky looked at his mother and gave her a hug. He was really glad he had decided to tell the truth and take responsibility for his actions. He wanted his mother to trust him and know he wouldn't lie to her. Besides, he promised himself, he really had learned a lesson. He would never again be so careless when he vacuumed.

⚠ Discussion Questions

1. What was Corky's mistake? (He was careless and accidentally broke a lamp.)

2. Did Corky follow the advice that you suggested?

3. Would it have been a mistake if Corky had lied? (Yes) Why? (It would have been another mistake.)

4. How did Corky's mother react? (She was upset but was proud Corky told the truth.)

5. What did Corky learn about making mistakes? (He learned that when he got angry he accidentally broke things but that he needed to take responsibility for his actions and learn from his mistake.)

6. Tell about a time you made a mistake and what you did about it.

7. Tell about a time somebody else made a mistake and didn't take responsibility for it and you were blamed for it.

🏃 Activities

1. Draw a picture of Corky telling his mother what happened to the lamp.

2. Print "We can learn from our mistakes" on your paper. (Teacher prints words on board for students to copy.)

🧎 Role Play

What should you do after making the following mistakes . . .

1. You and Amber were walking home and were so busy talking you made a wrong turn and got lost.

2. After school you accidentally took Dalton's ball home, instead of yours.

3. You put your sister's glass figurine on the edge of the table and it got knocked onto the floor.

4. You wanted to win a card game so badly that you cheated.

5. At Toby's house, she had two beautiful new Barbies (or Ninjas) and you wanted one. You hid it under your coat and took it home.

6. You got angry with your older brother outside so you came storming in the door and slammed your little sister's finger in the door.

7. You're angry with your sister so you tattle on her.

8. You spilled your soda on the living room rug and lied about it.

9. Shay has a toy you want to play with so you grab it away from her and it breaks.

10. You tell Kelsy that if she doesn't play what you want to play that you're going home.

☑ **Lesson 24: Setting Goals**

Setting Goals – Setting goals is to plan for a
future wish, desire, or thing that we want.

To set a goal means to work for something that doesn't just happen but requires desire and planning. It means to be able to look ahead and have a dream for the future. You might want to get to know someone better, make a new friend, learn to print better, read a book, get along better with a sister or brother, or hit the ball better. During our lives we will have lots of dreams and goals. Some of them we can work on and have in a few days or weeks, like making a new friend. Other goals take a long time, like graduating from high school.

Directions: Read and discuss the introduction. Review responsible behavior and then ask students what being responsible has to do with setting goals. (It is our responsibility to set goals for ourselves and help plan for our future, rather than just letting things happen.) The teacher will ask students to name some of their important dreams and goals. Tell them that often our dreams can become goals. The teacher writes ideas on the board. Ask the students to take out a piece of paper and a pencil and set it aside. Tell the students to be thinking about one special dream or goal that is important to them. Tell students: "Let's imagine that it's a beautiful day and we're lying down in the soft, green grass in a meadow, with lovely flowers all around. We're looking up at the sky, feeling the warm sun on our face and watching the clouds drift by. Let's pretend they are dream clouds and each of us will pick the one that is the biggest and the fluffiest that can hold a special dream or goal."

*(The teacher will demonstrate how to draw a cloud and ask the students
to draw one or copy the next page for student use. Then the teacher tells
the students the following:)*

Each of you will draw a picture of your special goal inside the cloud. If you aren't sure what your goal is now, perhaps you could use one we listed on the board. Remember, goals do not always stay the same. We may change our goal or we may set a goal and achieve it; then we set a new goal to work on.

*(After giving students time to draw their goal, teacher
talks about ways to make the goal come true.)*

To make a dream goal come true, we must have a plan. This means we must figure out at least two things to do to achieve our goal. For instance, if our goal is to make a new friend, the two steps to reach this goal might be:

1. Tell a new friend your name.
2. Ask the friend if they want to swing with you.

Dream Cloud for Goal

Name _____

Steps to Reach Goal

1. _____

_____

_____

2. _____

_____

_____

(If needed, the teacher will give more guided practice on possible goals and the two steps to achieve them. Then, tell the students to write the goal in their dream cloud and write the two things they can do to reach the goal.)

🪁 Activities

1. Have students decorate their clouds.
2. Have each student come to the front of the class and tell about the goal and the steps they chose.
3. Have students draw a picture of themselves achieving an important goal.

⚠ Discussion Questions

1. Did you choose a goal that you could do in just a few days? (Call on students to tell about their short-term goal.)
2. Is your goal one that is going to take a long time? (Call on students to tell about their long-term goal.)

🧎 Role Play

How would you take responsibility to plan for the following goals . . .

Have students role play or tell a two-step plan for the following goals.

1. Improve kicking the ball farther when playing kickball.
2. Stop fighting with your brother or sister.
3. Be a fireman when you grow up.
4. Learn how to ride a bike.
5. Pass first grade.
6. Learn to read better.
7. Help other friends more.
8. Make friends with the new neighbor.
9. Be an airplane pilot when you grow up.
10. Buy a new toy.

Appendix A
How to Make Sock Puppets

1. Teacher or students provide enough crew-type socks of the appropriate size to fit students' hands. Post pictures of the characters so students can see what they look like while making the puppets. It is recommended that each student have a sock to work with even if some characters will be duplicated. Remember to have at least one black sock (for Lucky Lambkin), one yellow sock (for Cherry Chicken), one gray sock (for Ted Turkey), and several brown ones (for Doolee and Daisy Dog, Corky Colt, Susie Squirrel, etc.). The others can be white or various colors.

2. Students can either make the puppets in class or the teacher may ask them to do it at home. If made at school, the teacher should arrange to have some adult helpers present. Students should each have a special character for their puppet but should be made to understand that they may not always be using that character but will share and/or trade them with other students.

3. If making the puppets in class, it will take about an hour for puppet construction and the teacher should have the following materials available: various shades of ribbon and yarn for hair and hair ribbons; black paper or inexpensive "wiggle" eyes available at craft stores, red paint for mouths; yellow felt for beaks; white cotton for fur; string and florist wire (or pipe cleaners) for whiskers and ears; glue that will attach paper, etc. to stockings; pins to attach items to socks, and textile paint or fabric for making features.

4. Assign students a character. They should put a sock on one hand and determine where the face will go and have the teacher or adult helper mark it. Remember, mouths will have upper and lower jaws or beaks as students use their thumbs for the lower jaw and fingers for upper jaw. Students should cut out facial features from the paper (or they may use paint or markers to make the features). To see how the features look, teacher or adult helper pins them on the stockings. Then students glue features in place, coloring with paints or markers as necessary.

5. Most characters' ears can be made by squeezing some of the sock into the proper shape and tying with string or gluing pipe cleaners on the socks. Rabbit ears can be made using pipe cleaners or florist wire and gluing white paper to the wire before anchoring it to the sock.

6. Students pick appropriate ribbons, yarn, or cotton for hair. Ribbon may be curled using scissors (like curling ribbon for wrapping presents). After "hair" is glued on, ribbons or tiny paper or felt hats may be glued onto hair.

7. Students may be creative in depicting their characters and add more color or innovations to their puppets. A main consideration is that the puppets be sturdy as they need to be stored at school and usable for many lessons. At the end of the year, students may want to take their character puppets home.

Appendix B
Resource Sheet 1

"I Am Special" Song
(Sing to "Brother John" tune)

I am special.
I am special.

So are you.
So are you.

Always remember.
Always remember.

This is true.
This is true.

Appendix B
Resource Sheet 2

"I" Messages Formula

I feel   _____

when   _____

because   _____.

    Give examples how "I" Messages fit into the formula. (I feel *hurt* when *you don't talk to me* because I think *you don't like me.* I feel *sad* when *you won't let me play* because *I don't have anyone to play with.*)

Appendix B
Resource Sheet 3

Steps to Problem-Solving

1. If you are angry, take three deep breaths and count to 10.

2. Each person states the problem. (No interrupting, name calling, or physical contact.)

3. Name some solutions (together).

4. Choose a solution that is fair (win-win).

5. Do the solution.

Appendix C
Responsibility Contract

To be signed after the first-grade curriculum has been taught.

I, _____ , am committed to learning how to be a kind, considerate, and responsible person with good character by learning to do the following things:

- I will always remember I am special.
- I believe everyone is special and will listen to what they say and give them respect.
- I am a good friend.
- I am honest.
- I solve problems peacefully.
- I can cope (make do) with whatever I need to do.
- I am always ready to learn.
- I make good choices and decisions.
- I have goals and work on them.
- I am responsible for my own actions, even when I make a mistake.

_____

Student's signature   Date

_____

Parent's signature (optional)   Date